Turning

FINANCIAL
PLANNING

Right-Side Up

JEFFREY SMALL

Turning
FINANCIAL
PLANNING
Right-Side Up

ADVISORS' ACADEMY
PRESS

TURNING FINANCIAL PLANNING RIGHT-SIDE UP

Published by
ADVISOR'S ACADEMY PRESS
Pompano Beach, Florida

ISBN 978-0-9975441-2-1
Ebook ISBN 978-0-9975441-3-8

FIRST EDITION

Book Design by Neuwirth & Associates
Jacket design by Tim Green

Manufactured in the United States

10 9 8 7 6 5 4 3 2 1

To my wife, Heather, and my three beautiful children, Jordan, Victoria (Tori), and Lily.

My wife gave me the privilege of naming our first daughter. I named her Victoria, which is the Latin name for "victory," and she loves winning. Victoria shares the same ideals that I want for my clients. I want them to win the inside game at investing and to modernize their money to reflect the current state of the markets. It has to be based on their needs and goals married with what is capable in today's investing environment, so they may achieve a better-than-average rate of return. If your investment advisor is long in the market and thinks risk is okay, you need to find a new advisor.

Why should you do that? Because the next eight years will not be like the last eight years in the markets. So, what do you do now? You must work with an advisor who will educate you on how to calculate your net rate of return going forward and reduce your stock-market risk. Easier said than done, but you must find an income-centered or income-centric advisor who can educate you on the universe of income-generating options that have the ability to earn between 4 to 7 percent on an annualized basis. There are many reasons to choose this path and avoid market risk—most of which I mention in this book.

JEFFREY SMALL

Contents

Introduction   1

1   Morally Bankrupt: How WALL STREET KILLED THE
AMERICAN DREAM AND WHAT YOU CAN DO ABOUT IT   7

2   The Art of Financial Self-Defense   27

3   Why You Should Get Out of the Market   51

4   The Importance of Yield in the Age of QE   99

5   The Goldilocks Zone: FIVE PERCENT IS
THE MAGIC NUMBER   119

6   Making Social Security Work for You   137

7   To Sell or Not to Sell: THE PROBLEM WITH REAL ESTATE   147

Conclusion   157

Turning

FINANCIAL PLANNING

Right-Side Up

Introduction

I HATE GAMBLING. DON'T get me wrong, I enjoy playing cards, rolling the dice, and spinning the roulette wheel just as much as the next guy. If you've ever been to Vegas, you understand it's a fun experience—and an addictive one at that if you're not careful. I just don't like throwing my money away. And at this stage in my life, there isn't a lot of money that I'm willing to risk losing. It's just not worth it. And after a certain age, frankly, it stops being fun, which is kind of the whole point.

But there's another reason why I avoid the practice. Casino games are all designed with one purpose in mind—to take in more money than they give out. Otherwise, the casino goes out of business. After all, if everyone could be a winner, they wouldn't stay open very long at all.

That's why each game is designed to stack the odds in the casino's favor. No matter what game you choose to play, the odds of the casino winning your money are greater than the odds of you winning theirs.

Put another way—the house always wins.

Investing is no different.

When you play the stock market, you assume that over the long run, you'll make money on your investments. The conventional wisdom paraded on Wall Street is that stocks are a sure thing—they always go up.

That may be true over the course of one's lifetime. But we only have one life. And while stocks may indeed go up over the long term, it doesn't change the fact that in any given year, the market can crash 20, 30, even 50 percent or more. It happened in 2000 and again in 2008.

With the market at all-time highs, investors are worried it could happen again. And yet, something remarkable has happened.

After the market went virtually nowhere for the better part of two years, on November 8, 2016, the election of Donald J. Trump to the office of the U.S. presidency ignited one of the greatest periods of market sentiment the world has ever seen. Investors went from being extremely cautious to insatiably greedy.

And yet, nothing has radically changed. Corporate earnings are still trending down. Interest rates remain at all-time lows. Inflation continues to be weak. The fundamentals haven't changed.

In other words, the market has rallied higher based on the *hopes* that with a new administration in the White House, things are going to get better.

It's possible they might.

It's possible they might not.

I'm here to tell you—it doesn't matter either way.

Just like gambling causes heartburn after a certain age, so does investing. That's because the stock market is no different than a casino. You pull the lever and hope for a positive result. The more it works in your favor, the more you think a one-off event like 2000 and 2008 can never happen again. Your financial planner will tell you the same thing—stocks always go up. And while you may indeed have the money to play the slots, let me ask you: can you make up for lost time, knowing it could take up to 10, 15, or 20 years just to break even if your bet goes wrong?

History proves this exact scenario can take place. That's why conventional wisdom—the kind you get from financial planners, investment analysts, and talking heads—states you should never have more than half of your money at risk in the market.

Me? I say zero.

Why put as much as half of your money at risk when you don't have to?

But Jeff, how can I expect to make a reasonable rate of return if I'm not willing to lose money?

My response: since when did losing money have anything to do with making it? How does that even make sense?

I get it. Wall Street says you can't make money without risk.

I'm here to tell you: it's not true.

The average retiree or pre-retiree understands at some level that, as you age, you should gradually reduce your exposure to the market. You can be more aggressive when you're young. After you've built up your nest egg with stocks, you switch to more defensive investments like bonds or even mutual funds. But there's more to investing than just stocks, bonds, and mutual funds. There are investments out there that Wall Street hasn't told you about that can hand you a significant return on your money, each year, while keeping your principle intact.

Wall Street doesn't want you to know about these investments because it doesn't get them paid.

But these investments are my bread and butter, and in the following pages I'm going to pull back the curtain to what I have found to be the best strategies for most people approaching retirement age. And besides, you shouldn't have to live as a pauper. These strategies can set you up for a lush and full retirement. And as you'll discover, they typically pay you more, in the form of interest and dividends, than if you had just kept your money in stocks, common stocks, and stock mutual funds.

To be clear, this isn't a book against Wall Street. My goal isn't to expose some deep-seated conspiracy in the financial planning industry. I've worked on both sides of the street. The people who work for these firms are good people, usually. They just happen to work in a bad system.

Rather, this book is about showing you there's a better, safer way to invest than what you've been told—one that will still grow your money well into retirement beyond what a standard "buy and hold" approach can get you.

Ask anyone of my clients. They'll tell you—it's possible.

While most financial planners peddle products to keep you in the market at any cost, I've built my career around providing *ethical* financial planning for retirees and those about to retire. In fact, my firm, Arbor Financial, is a member in good standing with The National Ethics Association, an honor I do not take lightly.

THE ONLY FINANCIAL PLANNING BOOK YOU NEED

I wrote this book with a single purpose in mind: to distill all the information in the financial planning industry—some of which is good, but most of which is bad—and create one, easy-to-read guide you can use to take control of your financial life.

As I'll reveal in the opening chapters, the financial planning industry—from the big firms to the charming and often well-intentioned financial advisors who work for them—are unable to advocate for you in the way that you need. Much of the information and guidance they provide is not only false, it's dangerous. To them, it doesn't matter whether the investments they select for you make you money or not. It doesn't even matter if you lose money. They collect their salaries and their fees either way. Said differently, the house *always* wins. They have zero skin in the game. And that, unfortunately, means they can't be trusted.

That begs the question. If you can't trust the professionals whose job it is to set you on a path to financial prosperity, who *can* you trust?

That's the question I've asked myself for 30 years as I've sought to be that person, offering my clients financial counsel they can trust. And it's the same question I asked myself before I started this book.

The fact is, there is a massive need in the market for good, honest financial wisdom. The media reports whatever keeps their ratings up. Similarly, financial advisors recommend strategies that may not be in your best interest. Their priority is to stay in business. It's not to prepare you for retirement, though they'll do their best to make you think otherwise.

This, to some extent, is the goal of any business—do whatever it takes to keep the money coming in. It's also very short sighted.

I have found that in the long run, it is more beneficial to advocate for my client's best interest—to invest in my clients' future. This might mean recommending a lower cost product that keeps more money in my client's pocket and puts less in mine. But it also means that those clients will stick with me for the long haul, because I deliver returns that are generally more stable and income they can count on.

Fact is, we're in a time when we need good financial information and even better financial advice, but we're not getting it. That's a huge problem. Life expectancy is longer. Medical costs are rising. It's a question whether Social Security will be around the way we expect it in the next 5 to 10 years.

To make matters worse, markets are rocky and unpredictable. It's almost too much for any one person to make sense of. We need help to make sense of it all. But the information that enters our homes to help us in this effort, whether through the mail, TV, radio, or the Internet, is dubious at best. "Fake news" has become a household phrase. The smiling investment guy in the suit offering his advice may not be any better. As I'll show you, he isn't.

All of this goes to explain why I wrote this book. You need better advice than your professional financial advisor or broker can offer you. You need to break out of the nonstop spin machine and get advice that can set you up for a prosperous retirement, one where you're not counting your pennies and are able to maintain the lifestyle you desire.

I wrote this book to turn your financial life upside down—or should I say, *right-side up*. My goal for you is that after you read this book, you'll have a clear picture of the best resources and opportunities you need to right the course of your financial life.

This is a mission I've been on my entire career, and I've spent much of the past three decades teaching thousands of clients what I call "the art of financial self-defense." We're told to take care of our minds and bodies, and we can only do these things ourselves. And yet we leave our most precious resource—our livelihood—in the hands of industry professionals who don't take the time to fully analyze our financial situation.

They don't have your best interests in mind.

I, on the other hand, work to create a complete picture of my client's financial life before we allocate a penny of funds to a single investment. Part of that means putting the client's needs first.

This book will provide you with the resources and opportunities you need to do just that, to put your interests above all else. That is, after all, what financial planning is supposed to be all about. It will clear up many of the misconceptions that put people in harm's way, and provide you with a clear view to the best viable options.

Yours to a long and prosperous retirement,

Jeffrey Small

1

Morally Bankrupt

How Wall Street Killed the American Dream and What You Can Do About It

THERE'S A MOMENT when every teenager comes to the unfortunate conclusion that he's not a child anymore. For me, that moment came the day of my sixteenth birthday. Growing up in my family, birthdays were pretty typical—presents, dinner with the family—except this time, my father said he wanted to "talk" after dinner, just the two of us. I asked if anything was the matter. He said everything was fine. He wanted to talk to me "just for a second."

My mind started spinning. Had I forgotten one of my chores? Had something happened in the family? Was my father losing his job?

Turns out, it was none of those things.

We stepped outside on the deck of my childhood home, and when it was just the two of us, my father looked me square in the eye and asked that question every boy dreads.

"Jeff, what do you want to *do* with your life?"

I felt all the gravity that came with that question. I had just turned sixteen. I was becoming a man. I had to think about whether I wanted to go to college. What kind of career I would have. Whether I would someday be able to support a family of my own. If I'd want to retire someday.

After a minute had passed, my father asked if I was going to answer his question.

I had to give him an answer. So, I looked right back at him and said what I can guarantee no sixteen-year-old in America has ever said to his father.

"Dad, I'm going to be a financial advisor."

I'm not sure where I originally got the idea to enter this field. All I knew is that I always had a knack for math and that I wanted to help people. And I figured everyone needs money. So I decided my job should be to help people make the most out of theirs. Becoming a financial advisor made the most sense.

Unfortunately, by time I graduated from college, got licensed and certified, and got a job working for one of the big financial firms, I realized that helping people make the most out of their money was far from the goal of this profession.

It didn't take long for me to reach that conclusion, either.

Every Friday morning at that big financial firm I worked for, the entire team gathered for our weekly sales meetings—and that's exactly what it was, a "sales" meeting.

These meetings weren't about teaching us to analyze a client's financial situation and select the best path for them. It wasn't about teaching us how to perform the kind of service you'd expect from a person who calls himself a "financial advisor."

Rather, they gathered us all into a room with a single objective—to teach us which products they wanted us to sell, and how we should sell them.

If they had asked us to sell bell weather products that could perform well in different market conditions, it would have been fine. But these products weren't designed to do that, and in my opinion, some were absolutely terrible.

Our goal was to sell high-risk, high-cost products—typically mutual funds—that, at best, matched the performance of the market, or, as was usually the case, underperformed the markets drastically. Not only were these funds expensive, they often failed to meet the exact objective that they were designed for. Years later, these were the same kinds of products that forced millions of Americans to say goodbye to retirement when they crashed in 2000 and again in 2008. Except this was the 1980s. Even then, I could tell it didn't make sense to sell high-risk, high-cost products to our clients when there was an entire universe of options that might suit them better—options that were more affordable, and safer too.

Immediately I had a crisis of faith. I didn't get into this industry to sell to people. I certainly didn't get into it to sell them products they didn't need, or that, God forbid, might actually hurt them.

I got into it to genuinely help people. I wanted to show people how, with precise action, they could make the American Dream real again.

So, one day, I quit.

After I had acquired enough experience to be credentialed, I quit my prestigious career as a glorified salesman at one of America's top financial firms and went to work on my own.

I decided that if I was going to be a financial advisor, I had to do it the right way—the honest way, which as far as I'm concerned is the only way that matters.

Before I continue, I want to reiterate a point I made in the introduction. This book is NOT about exposing some deep cover-up in the financial planning industry—but the problems that I'm about to highlight do exist within most of our country's firms, many of which you would recognize as household names.

Rather, this book is about teaching people how to turn their financial lives upside down, or should I say, *right-side up*. And part of that means realizing that the exact institutions that were designed to help you can hurt you.

From my experience, most of the advisors working for these firms are good, well-intentioned people. They pay their taxes. They coach Little League. They go to church on Sunday.

The problem is they're caught in a bad system—one that, unfortunately, does more harm than it does good.

This is an important point. At the big financial firms, your advisor is not allowed to select a course that is best suited to you. He is only allowed to pitch a handful of pre-selected products his boss has given the "all clear" to sell. And that's the financial industry's fatal flaw: there is zero consumer advocacy. What I mean by that is, the guy who's supposed to have your back, actually doesn't. He isn't allowed to advocate for you, to teach you the best path to maximize the probability that you enjoy a lush and full retirement.

And it isn't his fault. The financial planning industry exists for a single purpose. It's not to educate you. It's not about providing you a service. It's not even about preparing you for retirement. The financial planning industry's sole objective is to keep the financial planning industry going. It's about making sure those people who work for the industry, at the end of the day, still have jobs.

To some extent, I'm sure you've already realized this for yourself.

Here's an analogy. Let's say you go into an auto dealership with the intention of buying a used car. Buying a used car makes sense. After the first couple of years of the car's life, it's depreciated so much that you can often find a perfectly good car with low mileage for as little as half the price than if you had bought the thing new. Buying a used car is good financial common sense.

But the dealer has something else in mind. He doesn't want to sell you a used car. He wants to sell you a brand spanking new one with all the bells and whistles, because that's where he gets his commission.

Ask yourself: have you ever walked into a dealership, and the sales representative never asked what your budget was? Never so much as asked whether you even wanted a new car in the first place?

Or, have you ever gone in with the intention of buying a used car, told the dealer you want a used car, and they won't even so much as show you a used vehicle because their goal is to sell you a new one?

It's the same thing in the financial industry.

At the end of the day, that salesman cannot feel first-hand the financial burden you carry when you decided to purchase that shiny new piece of metal in your driveway, or that high-cost mutual fund that, coincidentally or not, can be just as poor an investment for your long-term retirement plans as buying a brand new Mustang. The salesman will never know that the financial decision he pressured you into will force you to cut corners on your financial goals. And the worst part?

It doesn't matter. He still got his commission. It doesn't matter if it was the right thing to do. So long as he got paid.

It's a sad reality: in the financial industry, people aren't held as accountable as they should be. Have you ever thought it odd that not one of the crooks who created the financial products that caused the housing meltdown in 2007 was sent to prison, even though that meltdown turned into a full-blown financial crisis, destroyed the retirement of millions of Americans, and cost people their jobs? Did it not also seem off that the government bailed out these crooks on the taxpayers' dime?

It does now. But to them, it doesn't matter how many people lose money or who gets hurt or who has to foot the bill. And it doesn't matter because most firms aren't incentivizing these people to sell a product that makes good financial sense.

So, Wall Street continues to peddle the age-old advice "buy and hold always wins." Shovel as much money into the market as you can, and hold on for the ride. Overtime, the market always—*always*—goes up.

And they're right. Historically, the market has always gone up over a long enough timeframe.

The market recovered after the Great Depression. It recovered after the inflationary crisis of the 1970s. And it recovered after the 2000 technology bust and the 2008 financial crisis.

But the long-term view is just one such perspective.

Over a shorter timeframe—the kind that actually matters to your financial goals—the reality is much different.

THE MARKET ALWAYS GOES UP,
BUT THAT'S JUST HALF THE STORY

Case in point: after the Dow Jones Industrial Average, or "Dow," peaked at 381 on September 3, 1929, it took 25 years, or until November 23, 1954 to reach that peak again.

Imagine if you had poured all your money into the top at the age of 40—the peak of your career and your spending power. You would have lived in fear all the way up until age 65, the age of retirement, wondering if you'd ever recover, and wondering if you'd ever have to suffer a blow like that to your finances again.

Tell that to any financial advisor who says "buy and hold" always wins.

The 1970s were a milder period, but still painful for investors, retirees, and those entering retirement. The market was virtually flat over the course of the decade. However, the Dow crashed roughly 50 percent in the two years between 1973 and 1974.

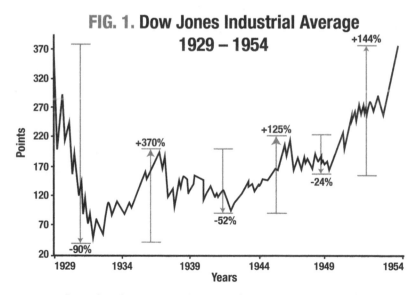

Source: http://www.macrotrends.net/1319/dow-jones-100-year-historical-chart

While the market eventually recovered by the end of the decade, it was no less painful to watch as half your money vanished. And the psychological toll was no less severe. People wondered if they'd ever be able to retire.

Then something incredible happened.

The market went on a seemingly endless bull market. From 1982 to 1999, investors pocketed a 1,238 percent return on their money, as the S&P 500, the standard benchmark index, rose from 112 on January 1, 1982 to 1,498 on January 1, 2000. It was the single greatest bull market to date. More millionaires and billionaires were minted than at any point in our nation's history.

People thought the party would never end.

Then it did.

By January 1, 2000, the market had become so overbought and so "irrationally exuberant," to borrow a phrase from then-chairman of the Federal Reserve Alan Greenspan, that the market entered the most severe bear market in a quarter century. For those unfamiliar with the

FIG. 2. S&P 500 in the 1970s

Source: https://finance.yahoo.com/quote/%5EGSPC/history?period1=277200&period2=315810000&interval=1mo&filter=history&frequency=1mo

terminology, a bear market is a period when stocks and other financial assets go down 20 percent or more over a long enough period of time. A bull market, by contrast, is a period when stocks go up.

But this wasn't any 20 percent down market.

By mid-2002 when the carnage ended, the market had lost half its value—a 50 percent loss of investor's money. Once again, investors and retirees all over wondered if they'd ever recover.

They did. In 2002, the market began showing signs of life. Investors started to have hope again. By 2007, the market had fully recovered.

Only then, the market entered an even more monstrous bear market, losing 57 percent of its total value in a little more than a year. Two massive bear markets, back to back, in less than a decade. This time, it wasn't until 2013 before the market recovered.

Think about that. Between 2000 and 2013, the market went through no growth. Zero. Zilch. Nada. Thirteen years of heartache with nothing to show for it.

FIG. 3. S&P 500 Index

Source: https://finance.yahoo.com/quote/%5EGSPC/history?ltr=1

And yet, Wall Street continues to preach "buy and hold always wins." Does it?

As I write today, the market is up more than 50 percent from its 2000 high. Sure enough, buy and hold works over the long haul.

But was it worth it?

Do you *feel* 50 percent richer?

Of course not.

Wall Street wants you to believe that the market grows, on average, 8 to 10 percent every year. They're right. Historically, that's how much the market has risen per year.

And yet, between 2000 and 2013, the market experienced zero growth.

And between 2000 and 2017, it averaged just 2 percent growth per year.

Nowhere near the 8 to 10 percent growth Wall Street likes to throw at you.

So, why does the average person continue to put their money in stocks and mutual funds after they've been burned so many times? Albert Einstein called this the definition of insanity doing the same thing over and over again and expecting different results.

The answer: they feel like they have no choice.

And they've been given bad information.

That's because high-risk, high-cost products such as stocks and mutual funds are often the only options Wall Street has presented to them.

They don't want to let you know there are more conservative investment vehicles that almost never lose their value and still pay a respectable dividend. (Later on in this book, I'll tell you exactly what those investment vehicles are.)

They don't want to let you know that by a certain age, some of these options will actually leave you richer than buying the stocks and mutual funds they worship so dearly.

Why doesn't Wall Street tell you about them? It's simple. They don't make as much money selling you those financial vehicles. Just like a car dealer doesn't make as much money selling you a used car as he does selling you a new one.

The used car may not be as flashy. It may not turn heads on the road. But it makes better financial sense. Perhaps more importantly, it will help you sleep better at night.

Sadly, Wall Street doesn't care how well you sleep. That isn't their business model. Their business model is to make as much money as humanly possible. Selling you low-cost, low-risk products doesn't cut it. Subjecting you to risky assets that could leave you 50 percent poorer overnight—that's how they make their money.

That is simply unacceptable. And that's why I have dedicated my entire career to teaching Americans that there is a better way.

Wall Street wants you to believe that the only way to make money is to put at least half of your money at risk in things like common stock and stock mutual funds. I say the number should be far less than half. And I wouldn't be heartbroken if you don't want to have any of your money in these types of things, especially when you factor in the market's current valuation. In this book, I'll show you why the market doesn't support taking on any risk at today's levels.

That's why Americans today need to radically change their perspective when it comes to investing for retirement. The old way of doing things doesn't work anymore. That buy and hold is the only way to go is a lie that's been sold to you by Wall Street, by politicians, by the media, and by your own financial advisor who, supposedly, has your best interest in mind.

WHAT WALL STREET'S FEES COST YOU

This isn't just the case for the typical salaried American. It's the case for everyone—from the NASA engineer, to the business owner, to the former banker. Each and every one of them have accounts that have unnecessary fees, non-performing assets, undue risk, and hidden costs.

I've seen it first-hand.

Many of the potential clients that have walked into my office are unaware of the various fees their investment strategy is costing them. They might understand that the mutual funds their broker put them in, charge a fee, but they often don't know how much. And even fewer realize that their broker charges a fee on top of what the mutual fund charges. Even if they are aware, in my experience, they're not sure how much those fees are.

They're also unaware that most mutual funds fail to match the overall market's performance. Many of them are even down when the overall market is up.

How can that be possible? It all has to do with the way these funds are set up. Many of them are just bad products with too much money in bad sectors of the market that lose their investors' money.

But even though these clients are highly educated—successful businessmen and women who are highly respected in their fields—they blindly put their faith in these financial advisors who tell them the market always goes up, trusting them to manage their money for maximum growth. They figure if they can't do it, who can?

Here's a worst case scenario that I've seen all too often:

1. The client is getting charged high fees they're unaware of.
2. Factoring in inflation, their money is often going backward as the mutual fund underperforms.
3. The client, once retired, withdraws money from these accounts— typically 4 percent or so each year—for living expenses, without understanding the real risk of running out of money.

It's a triple whammy. These clients are losing money in three different ways. It's a recipe for disaster.

Unfortunately, this scenario happens far too often. Take it from a guy who's worked 33 years in the industry.

Here's an actual example of a client who recently came to me.

The client—let's call him Richard—came to me with a portfolio worth $778,154, just over three quarters of a million dollars—a respectable amount he'd worked hard for and was ready to retire on.

Richard was 65 years old. He was about to quit his job, begin collecting Social Security, and live out his golden years—what the American Dream is all about. He asked me what he could expect his portfolio to look like in 15 years.

It wasn't good.

After we ran the numbers, the look on Richard's face was one of pure surprise. I had an idea it would be bad, but I didn't know how bad until we ran the actual numbers. Richard? The poor guy had no idea.

Present Value: $778,154.00						Number of Years: 16	
Average Yield: 5.00%			Fees: 2.00%			Actual Yield: 2.90%	
YEAR	VAR. RATE	ANNUAL PAYMENT	COST FREE ACCT. E.O.Y.	ANNUAL MGT. FEE		NET ACCOUNT VALUE E.O.Y.	ACCOUNT DIFFERENCE
1	5.00%		817,062	(16,341)		800,720	(16,341)
2	5.00%		857,915	(16,815)		823,941	(33,973)
3	5.00%		900,811	(17,303)		847,836	(52,975)
4	5.00%		954,851	(17,805)		872,423	(73,428)
5	5.00%		993,114	(18,321)		897,723	(95,420)
6	5.00%		1,042,801	(18,852)		923,757	(119,044)
7	5.00%		1,094,941	(19,399)		950,546	(144,395)
8	5.00%		1,149,688	(19,961)		978,112	(171,576)
9	5.00%		1,207,172	(20,540)		1,006,477	(200,695)
10	5.00%		1,267,531	(21,136)		1,035,665	(231,866)
11	5.00%		1,330,907	(21,749)		1,065,699	(265,208)
12	5.00%		1,397,453	(22,380)		1,096,605	(300,848)
13	5.00%		1,467,325	(23,029)		1,128,406	(338,919)
14	5.00%		1,540,692	(23,697)		1,161,130	(379,562)
15	5.00%		1,617,726	(24,384)		1,194,803	(422,924)

Figure 4 Source: Jeff Smalls

The initial picture is a good one.

Assuming 5 percent portfolio growth each year, Richard could expect his money to more than double over 15 years, from roughly three quarters of a million dollars, to $1,617,726.

This is where it starts to get bad.

Next we had to factor in living expenses. We determined Richard would need to take out $37,000 every year to cover his costs. Fortunately, his home was paid off—lots of retirees aren't so lucky. All Richard had to worry about was bills, like groceries and healthcare, and travel costs to go on vacation and visit his three children.

With 5 percent portfolio growth, the account was virtually unchanged. After pulling out $37,000 every year, that 5 percent growth was enough to keep his accounts above water. His portfolio had actually *grown* $1,255 over the last 15 years, from $778,154 to $779,399—nothing to write home about, but he hadn't lost money, either. That's a victory in itself.

But that wasn't the whole story.

Richard had to take into account that his broker charged a 1 percent fee every year. His mutual funds charged a 1.1 percent fee on top of that. Suddenly, his 5 percent annual return was cut nearly in half to just 2.9 percent.

At that rate, in 15 years, Richard would have to fork over exactly $287,454, a third of his money, as his account shrunk from $778,154 to just $491,854—a 37 percent loss of his money.

Even then, Richard was in better shape than most. In 15 years, he would still have almost half a million dollars to his name at 80 years old. But before he had factored in his costs, it had been over three times that much. After costs, expenses, and fees, he would have lost $1,125,872.

It didn't make Richard mad.

It made him *furious*.

It should make you furious as well. Because the exact same thing is likely happening to you.

Granted, Richard didn't have to worry about running out of money. By age 80, he would still have half a million dollars to work with. But if he went on to live *another* 10 or 15 years—entirely possible as lifespans seem to increase with each passing year—he would be in real trouble. And he certainly wouldn't be able to leave nearly as much money for his children's inheritance. In short, his legacy would all but disappear.

But there was another, even more dangerous scenario we had to consider.

What if in that 15-year period the market entered another tailspin like in 2000 and 2008?

A bear market, by definition, is a 20 percent loss to the overall market. But as the last two decades have proven, they can be far worse, as high as 50 percent and even 58 percent. Had you put your money di-

Present Value: $778,154.00					Number of Years: 16	
Average Yield: 5.00%			Fees: 2.00%			Actual Yield: 2.90%
YEAR	VAR. RATE	ANNUAL PAYMENT	COST FREE ACCT. E.O.Y.	ANNUAL MGT. FEE	NET ACCOUNT VALUE E.O.Y.	ACCOUNT DIFFERENCE
1	5.00%	-37,000	778,212	(15,564)	762,647	(15,564)
2	5.00%	-37,000	778,272	(15,239)	746,691	(31,581)
3	5.00%	-37,000	778,336	(14,904)	730,272	(48,064)
4	5.00%	-37,000	778,403	(14,559)	713,377	(65,026)
5	5.00%	-37,000	778,473	(14,204)	695,992	(82,481)
6	5.00%	-37,000	778,546	(13,839)	678,103	(100,444)
7	5.00%	-37,000	778,624	(13,463)	659,695	(118,929)
8	5.00%	-37,000	778,705	(13,077)	640,753	(137,952)
9	5.00%	-37,000	778,790	(12,679)	621,262	(157,528)
10	5.00%	-37,000	778,880	(12,269)	601,205	(177,674)
11	5.00%	-37,000	778,974	(11,848)	580,567	(198,406)
12	5.00%	-37,000	779,072	(11,415)	559,331	(219,742)
13	5.00%	-37,000	779,176	(10,969)	537,478	(241,698)
14	5.00%	-37,000	779,285	(10,510)	514,992	(264,292)
15	5.00%	-37,000	779,399	(10,038)	491,854	(287,545)

Figure 5 Source: Jeff Smalls

rectly into the Nasdaq during the tech boom, you would have suffered far worse and lost 80 percent of your money as tech stocks were completely obliterated.

But for Richard's purposes, we kept it simple. We assumed that in at least one of those 15 years, we could expect at least a 20 percent downturn. So, rather than make 5 percent that year, we replaced it with a 20 percent loss.

In that most conservative of scenarios, there would be no recovery. By the time he was 80 years old, Richard would only have $234,049 to his name. Less than a third of what he had started with.

And one loss year of only 20 percent is a pretty optimistic scenario.

I won't even show what would happen to Richard if his portfolio lost 30 percent, 40 percent, or even 50 percent of its value in any given year due to a market crash. But I'm sure you can get the idea.

Present Value: $778,154.00   Number of Years: 16

Average Yield: 3.44%   Fees: 2.00%   Actual Yield: 0.22%

YEAR	VAR. RATE	ANNUAL PAYMENT	COST FREE ACCT. E.O.Y.	ANNUAL MGT. FEE	NET ACCOUNT VALUE E.O.Y.	ACCOUNT DIFFERENCE
1	5.00%	-37,000	778,212	(15,564)	762,647	(15,564)
2	-20.00%	-37,000	592,969	(11,610)	568,908	(24,062)
3	5.00%	-37,000	583,768	(11,170)	547,333	(36,435)
4	5.00%	-37,000	574,106	(10,717)	525,133	(48,974)
5	5.00%	-37,000	563,962	(10,251)	502,288	(61,673)
6	5.00%	-37,000	553,310	(9,771)	478,782	(74,528)
7	5.00%	-37,000	542,125	(9,277)	454,593	(87,532)
8	5.00%	-37,000	530,381	(8,769)	429,704	(100,678)
9	5.00%	-37,000	518,050	(8,247)	404,092	(113,958)
10	5.00%	-37,000	505,103	(7,709)	377,738	(127,365)
11	5.00%	-37,000	491,508	(7,155)	350,619	(140,889)
12	5.00%	-37,000	477,233	(6,586)	322,714	(154,519)
13	5.00%	-37,000	462,245	(6,000)	294,000	(168,245)
14	5.00%	-37,000	446,507	(5,397)	264,453	(182,055)
15	5.00%	-37,000	429,983	(4,777)	234,049	(195,934)

Figure 6 Source: Jeff Smalls

WHAT WALL STREET'S FEES COST YOU

If you are anywhere close to retirement, or want to retire someday, this matters to you.

If you continue to play Wall Street's game, putting most or all of your money at risk in the hopes of making a few bucks, I promise, it can end quite badly. Historically, the average bull market lasts eight years. The current bull market began in 2009 when the market bottomed after the financial crisis. It's 2017. By historical averages, the next bear market could begin any day now. History has proven it's possible.

I mentioned before I don't like gambling. But I would bet every dollar I have to say the market will crash at least 20 percent at some point in the next 15 years.

I can practically guarantee it.

Of course, I can't put all the blame on Wall Street. If any high-ranking CEO of a Fortune 500 corporation or money management firm came out and said the market was on its last legs and we should all hunker down, get out of the market, and hoard all our cash, their investors would burn them at the stake.

Point is, it's no one individual person's fault. It's a systemic issue with no clear resolution.

Fortunately, I'm not the only one who thinks this way. That's why I founded Arbor Financial, and it's one of a very small number that have crafted our very own niche in the market to provide solid, honest financial advice to our clients. And I'm proud to say I have never had a client come to me and turn their back. The only people who leave my office are paranoid control freaks who can't trust anybody or who are afraid to try something different. But once I show them how much money I can earn for them in the form of interest and dividends compared to their current advisor, almost every client who has come to me, without fail, has made the switch. That's because I tell them exactly how it is. If they stay with their advisor, they will earn less income and take more risk. Eventually, there will be another market drop, and they will lose money. If they come to me, they will earn more consistent money in the form of income, with a lot less volatility risk. It's that simple.

At this point, you need to ask yourself a series of questions.

The first is, what is your financial situation? Do you have kids? Have they moved out? Are they in college? Have you paid off your car? Have your paid off your home? Should you downsize your home?

Next, ask yourself: how many income streams do I have? How long can I afford to defer Social Security payments (the longer you wait, the better, though it's not always that simple)?

Then, consider your medical costs. What are they? What could come up later? That's important. If you have a family history of serious medical conditions such as cancer, Alzheimer's, multiple sclerosis, dementia, or any other disease of that caliber, you want to make sure you have enough set aside that you can combat that illness to the best of your ability if it should come to that.

Now, consider this: when do you want to retire? Do you even want to? (Some people don't.)

Finally, do you want to be able to afford to maintain the same lifestyle you have today in your retirement, or are you willing to trim a few hedges? How much do you want to travel? And how much money do you want to be able to leave to your children?

There are a million and one different things to consider to create your individual retirement outlook. But it's worth taking the time to map everything out. Trust me—you'll thank me later. So will your spouse and your children.

Once you've done all that, it's time to have a serious talk with your financial advisor.

How well does he or she really know you and your financial situation? How satisfied are you with his or her performance? And before you started reading this book, were you even aware there was an alternative?

I can practically guarantee that if your financial advisor is associated with one of the big financial firms, he has been trained not to advocate for you. He has not been trained to show you a universe of products that might be better for you. He has only been trained to sell you a product his company wants him to sell. He has a script and he sticks to it.

Worse, he hasn't been taught how to do his or her own research like I have. That's a problem, because almost everyone in this industry uses the same distorted, watered-down information passed down from various billion-dollar industries.

Wall Street tells you stocks are a sure bet, whether the market's up 140 percent or down 30 percent. The media plays second fiddle. No one wants to watch a program saying the worst is yet to come. That stuff is reserved for blogs on the Internet, many of which aren't the least bit reputable. That's why financial programs bring their advertisers on air to support the hypothesis that stocks are strong, that the market will keep going up, and that if you haven't gone all in, you're missing out. It keeps the cash coming into their coffers.

Don't buy it. I'm here to tell you, the companies that sell investments are not your friends, the media doesn't know what it's talking about, and your financial advisor is not acting in accord with your best interests nearly to the extent you deserve.

I can help you fix it.

TURNING YOUR FINANCIAL LIFE RAFT RIGHT-SIDE UP

I hope after reading this chapter I've helped open your eyes to some of the conventional retirement strategies peddled by Wall Street and its media cronies. Even if you had a hunch something was amiss, I hope that now you have a clearer picture. There's a ton of misinformation out there, and I want you to be safe.

The truth is that if you abide by traditionally accepted standards of financial planning, you are sailing a financial ship with no course.

When a ship sails without a course, one of two things happen. You don't arrive at your destination. That, or you sink. You don't end up lucky and arrive where you intended. Life doesn't work that way.

Needless to say, that's not the outcome we want for our clients. And that's what separates us at Arbor Financial from the big institutions trying to steer you astray. Rather than sell one-size-fits-all cookie cutter solutions to every client who walks in our door, we scrutinize every detail of their financial life to custom fit the financial plan best suited to *them*.

You can't just take any path to retirement. There's only one path you can take, and that's the one that's right for you.

I understand that can be overwhelming to some people. There are so many options to consider. There are as many options as there are millions of Americans preparing for retirement. And our goal is to find nothing short of the very best financial road for that specific client. We consider every outcome, look over every detail, and leave no stone unturned.

Frankly, most clients aren't used to being treated that way. They're used to a financial manager giving them the same cookie-cutter advice they give to everyone else. The notion of providing a customized financial experience, unfortunately, seems to be a novel concept.

But there's a second part to selecting the right financial course for our clients, and it's the most important.

That is, we can't choose it for you.

That may come as a surprise. Many would think that only someone like me, with my background and experience as a financial planner and income specialist, has the proper education to make those kinds of decisions. But nothing is further from the truth.

The fact is, only you can decide the path that is best suited to you.

I can't make that decision for you. Frankly, no one can. I can provide you the resources and tools that are necessary to help you make the best decision you can possibly make, and that's exactly what I've achieved with hundreds of my clients. But ultimately, it is *your* decision. I can give you the best advice I've collected in my 30 years in the financial industry. But unless that advice applies directly to you and your unique situation, it's worthless. There is no one-size-fits-all approach to retirement.

That may frighten you. Don't let it. It should *empower* you. The right financial path is out there. It's just waiting for you to find it. I'll even help you do it.

Sure, not everyone wants to put in the work. Some people want others to tell them exactly what to do. That's not how I work. My goal is to educate my clients so they can play a direct role in their retirement and make the right financial decisions on their own. I'll be there to help see them through once they do.

I'll be the first to admit my style is different than most. Ours is the road less traveled. It's not the easiest road either. It does require a bit of work and for you to play an active role in your financial strategy. But it works. Here's why. Once I help a client choose the right financial course for them, something incredible happens.

They take *ownership* of it.

Suddenly, they start to see, clear as day, what their retirement will look like, and exactly how they'll get there. Every single one of them tells me it's like a light switch that turned on in a dark room. Retirement suddenly becomes more than just about quitting your job. It becomes about vacations with grandchildren. Time spent with loved ones. The time and resources you need to pick up hobbies you've long since forgotten. The peace of mind you need to let yourself relax and do the things that bring value to your life.

I have found that once people find the picture—what their best retirement looks like—they fully commit to it. And that, at the end of the day, is more valuable than any piece of advice I can offer.

That brings us to the next chapter.

2

The Art of Financial
Self-Defense

I HAVE THREE CHILDREN. One is five, one is seven, and the other is
eighteen. I don't know what it's like to grow up with a financial adviser for a father. My father was a general manager at a store that sold
carpet. He did well enough for himself, but he wasn't a certified financial adviser. He was a businessman, but just because you know business
doesn't mean you know investing.

Frankly, I'm glad my children get to have me as a father. Not just
because they're *my* children and I love them. I'm glad I'm their father
because I'll always be there to offer them sound financial advice thanks
to my profession.

I've already done this for my eighteen-year-old son. He understands
there's a cost to everything, and he also understands he has to choose
to do the right thing in life the same way that I choose to do the right
thing by our clients. That's why he turned down scholarships to play
college football. His goal was always to join the military after he graduated. He knew that if he was going to save his body for the military,
playing football at the college level for four years wasn't going to cut it.
The fact that he understands this makes me believe he'll do well for
himself. His body—like a retiree's net worth—is a resource that he can

either save or spend. By choosing to save it, he'll be able to spend it on the thing that matters to him most. It's a lesson in discipline I think we all could benefit from.

I think one of the greatest failures of the American school system is that we fail to teach our children this sort of discipline. Kids today don't understand cost. I would go so far to say that we don't teach them an ounce of financial literacy, and that we're raising a country of financial illiterates.

That's ironic when you think about it. The financial sector of America's economy is the largest in the developed world. And yet, our financial literacy rates are among the worst. We have the most money, and the worst understanding of money. How does that happen?

We teach our children how to multiply and divide, how to read, the difference between liquids and solids, etc. But we don't require them to learn critical survival skills that will actually help them survive, get a job, save for retirement, learn how to be happy, or become a productive member of society. We don't teach them how to change a tire, how to start a fire in the wilderness, or how to do their taxes—none of it. It's frightening.

Today, we have a generation of young people who are well-read and well-educated, but sadly don't understand the first thing about what it means to be an entrepreneur or how to survive in the economy. I think that's the root of our entitlement problems. The upcoming generation has had everything provided for them. They don't understand where money comes from. They think everything is free.

I could write an entire book just about that. But it's concerning from a financial-planning perspective, because when people don't understand the first thing about the economy, they're prone to every kind of misinformation I described in the last chapter. They become easily sold by people who know just a little bit more than they do. It's a chronic disease I call "financial blindness."

HELPING THE BLIND SEE

I know a thing or two about blindness. When my youngest daughter Lilly was born, the doctors said she would never see.

Lilly was born with a congenital eye disease called coloboma. It basically means her eyes didn't develop correctly while my wife was pregnant with her. In Lilly's case, it affected her optic nerve and her retina.

Her prognosis wasn't good.

The doctors assumed she would be handicapped her whole life. The likelihood of her seeing anything was low. She would have to learn to use her hands and her ears to guide her. The chances of her ever becoming an independent person were low. She would have to rely on people forever.

Or so the doctors thought.

What they failed to take into consideration is the sheer sense of will-power and determination that runs in our family.

Today, my daughter sees almost perfectly.

While she'll never see as well as her peers, or as she would if her eyes had developed normally, she sees well enough that it almost doesn't matter.

She goes to school. She reads books. She colors in the lines. She can work a mouse on a computer. She can do just about anything any other child can do.

We're incredibly fortunate.

The fact is, most children with Lilly's condition aren't so lucky. I could be wrong, but I attribute much of our good fortune to the fact that my wife and I never gave up on her. We didn't accept that she'd have to go through life with a crippling handicap.

In short, we were her *advocates*. My daughter was also fortunate to inherit her father's tenacity.

YOU NEED AN ADVOCATE

There's a lesson here when it comes to financial planning.

Most of the clients who come to me have suffered from financial blindness their whole lives. No one ever taught them how to color in the lines. No one ever even taught them where the lines were. A nice guy in a suit sold them on the idea that stocks always go up—that the game would work in their favor. No one ever told them that the house always wins. Anyone who's ever come to me has been burned by one financial adviser or gotten bad advice in the past.

They've had a lot of financial salesman. But they've never had a financial *advocate*.

No one has ever taken the time to show them what financial planning done right looks like. As it turns out, you don't have to buy stocks until the day you die hoping the market never turns south. Sooner or later, it always does. But there are ways to avoid that fate, but Wall Street has kept you blind to them.

Most of the clients who walk through my door for the first time have never found a home for their money. I have learned that no one has ever taken the time to help them open their eyes to alternative financial strategies. No one has ever told them there is a universe of alternative investments and pathways that may lead them to a richer and fuller retirement.

It's not their fault. Nobody ever taught them how to see these things. And it's difficult to see something if you don't know it's there in the first place.

A lot of people who come to me think they're financially stupid.

They're not.

You certainly aren't, either.

Most of us are simply the product of a culture that has not taught us *how* to prepare for retirement, only that we're supposed to.

Imagine if someone took you off the street and asked you to perform brain surgery. Obviously you'd fail. Not because you *couldn't* do it. But because you haven't gone through years and years of training and research. With the right amount of training and a small measure of talent, anyone can do just about anything.

You may have heard this story about the world-famous choreographer Gillian Lynne. She did works like *Cats* and *Phantom of the Opera*.

When Gillian was in grade school, she couldn't sit still. Not only that, but she couldn't concentrate, she kept getting up out of her seat, her homework was always late, and she would disrupt other kids in the classroom. Concerned she might be mentally ill, the teachers wrote home to Gillian's parents saying she might have a learning disorder. She had what doctors today might diagnose as ADHD.

Finally, Gillian's mother took her to see a specialist. The specialist watched Gillian from behind a one-sided mirror and turned on the radio. The moment he did, Gillian got to her feet and started moving.

The specialist turned to Gillian's mother and said, "Mrs. Lynne, your daughter isn't sick. She's a dancer."

So they enrolled her in a dance school full of people who, like Gillian, couldn't sit still.

And do you know what happened? Gillian went on to become one of the greatest dancers of her generation. When she could no longer dance, she switched to choreography and excelled in that too. Today, her work has been seen by millions and she has a net worth of several million dollars.

Someone else might have put her on medication at the age of eight and told her to sit still.

There's another story about how Albert Einstein's grade school teachers thought he was mentally retarded—the boy who would later become the world's greatest genius. It wasn't until he went to more challenging schools that he learned to behave himself and excel in his studies.

Imagine that. Two geniuses who, had they not had someone advocate for them and put them on the right path at an early age, might not have been as successful.

ADVOCATE, BUT ALSO EDUCATE

I understand we can't go back in time and set ourselves on the right path a little earlier. Hindsight is 20-20. But it's never too late to fix a mistake. As the old saying goes—better late than never. But the only way we can make sure we don't make the same mistakes we made in 2000 and 2008 is to learn from them and move forward. Einstein said the definition of insanity is doing the same thing over and over again and expecting different results.

That's why it's not only important that an advisor must advocate for their clients, they must also educate them. In my experience, folks can't see what their financial path should be until they've had an advocate work with them.

That's why I don't select the right financial course for my clients. I make them do it themselves—but only after I've taught them how.

Why do I do this?

Wouldn't it be easier if I just did it myself? Isn't that my job?

These are fair questions.

The reason I do this is because it's your retirement, not mine.

I don't want clients who hang onto my every word but don't take the time to actually learn anything. Financial ignorance leads to bad decisions. That's why it's important that I educate them how to select the right financial path for themselves. I don't want them to put blind faith in me like they might have with their last advisor. I want them to be able to think for themselves. After all, it's not *my* retirement at stake.

As a parent, I've had to learn how to raise kids who don't hang onto my every word. On the one hand, it's easier to be strict and tell them what to do in all things. It's more challenging to teach them how to behave for themselves. But once you instill that in them, they're better able to go out and become independent people.

It's the same when it comes to financial planning.

I have found that once I have helped educate my clients how to think for themselves and make their own decisions based on their financial needs, it makes a world of difference. Ultimately, I can never be as invested in your retirement as you are. When you are able to make educated choices about the exact financial strategies you need to have your best retirement, you become better able to advocate for *yourself*. And once you can do that, you become unstoppable. Nothing will stand in your way.

I call this practice: "the art of financial self-defense."

RETIREMENT IS ALL ABOUT INCOME

What exactly is the art of financial self-defense?

It's a discipline we teach to retirees and pre-retirees who come into our office. At its most basic level, it's about protecting your assets. It's financial self-protection. Pretty self-explanatory.

How we do it gets a little more complicated.

Basically, the art of financial self-defense means getting the most *income* you can from your money with the *least* amount of risk. The goal is to make money you can survive on while keeping your assets intact. Make more, spend less. It's that simple.

The investment world can basically be divided into two different types of people: those who invest for growth and those who invest for income.

Wall Street is the standard bearer for the pro-growth school of investing. They want you to believe that stocks always go up, and if you want to ride the growth train higher, you need to be willing to have a certain amount of your money at risk.

The problem is that risk is a double-edged sword. Sure, your assets may grow quicker from one year to the next. But when the market turns on you, it erases several years of those hard-earned gains.

I come from the pro-income school of investing.

An income investor, by his nature, is more conservative than his pro-growth peer. He wants to get the greatest amount of money for the least amount of risk. It's a matter of getting the most income you possibly can without depleting your assets. Ultimately, it's about keeping your money whole.

In a sense, income investors are like financial ninjas. Their goal is to get in, collect their income, and get out without a scratch.

Now don't get me wrong. There's nothing wrong with investing for growth. If you're a young investor who can afford to take a major financial hit, knowing the market will eventually recover before it's time for you to retire—by all means, roll the dice. If the market crashes, you have time to recover.

But after a certain age, investing for growth with anything more than a small percentage of your money doesn't make good financial sense.

LEARNING TO PUT GROWTH ASIDE

If you're 55 years old or above, you likely have already made significant strides toward your retirement. The worst thing that could happen is you put all your money in the market, the market crashes, and it takes you 25 years to make up for your losses. By then, you'd be 80 years old, your portfolio has never recovered because you had to withdraw some each year for living expenses, and you're almost out of money. It's a gamble. If you lose, you run out of money, and you lose everything.

Remember, the house always wins. If you play with fire, sooner or later, you're going to get burned.

That's why, by the time you turn 55 years old, it's important to switch to a *defensive* financial strategy that helps protect your assets from ever running out—the kind of financial strategy we practice at Arbor Financial.

Using our methods, you'll avoid a devastating market downturn that could cut your money in half. You'll also avoid excessive management fees that eat into your principle. And you'll earn some interest or dividends every year—not by swinging for the fences, but by targeting a consistent return that will help you grow and preserve your money for years and even decades to come.

You can't get that at the big Wall Street firms.

Their retirement plan comes pre-made and off the shelf.

Ours is not only custom fit, it's typically cheaper too.

THE RIGHT EDUCATION MAKES ALL THE DIFFERENCE

This gets at the problem with the traditional model of financial planning. The problem is that there is no education. Wall Street tells people what to buy and people buy it. But they seldom take the time to *educate* them *why* they should buy it. People assume these guys just know what they're talking about. That can get you in trouble.

Fact of the matter is, unless you're getting the right education, you can't make a good informed decision that will benefit your financial future.

It's that simple.

So, what we do with our clients is, we educate them about how they can protect and grow their assets closer to retirement to virtually eliminate the risk of running out of money.

This requires a different game plan.

Rather than stick to the same high-cost investment products people are used to, we show them the universe of options their financial advisor probably *hasn't* told them about.

Now you no longer have a salesperson just trying to get you to buy a product.

Now you have a financial professional advocating for your future.

Unfortunately, the average financial advisor is too busy peddling product to take the time to get to know their clients and do this. Frankly, many couldn't care less about what's best for their clients. They're not interested in their goals, their values, or their objectives. And they're certainly not interested in educating them to make informed decisions for themselves. To them, risk is the be all, and end all, because that's what gets them paid the most. They try to convince you that you cannot make money without risk. Let's face it, if everyone wanted to take absolutely *no* risk in their investments, the Wall Street machine would come to a screeching halt.

PLANNING FOR THE FUTURE

I'll illustrate this with a story.

In 2015 I had a client come to me. We'll call him David.

David entered my office in a wheelchair. Naturally, it was the first thing I noticed.

Before we even started talking, I began running calculations in my head. Whatever his condition was, I knew there was a financial cost that would have to be factored into his retirement plan. Any financial advisor worth his salt would know this.

I also knew, before David said so much as a word, that his previous managers had likely never discussed those costs with him because they probably didn't care.

I was right.

During our initial visit, David told me he had worked with two financial advisors before coming to see me. Both were from leading financial institutions—the big firms that represent the so-called "industry standard." David figured he was doing the right thing by working with two advisors instead of one. That way, he always had a second opinion.

I stopped him right there.

I didn't tell him that financial advisors peddle the same advice wherever you go, and that it didn't matter whether he had two advisers or three or an army of these guys.

Instead, I asked him a simple question.

"David, what's up with the wheelchair?"

I think he was surprised by the directness of my question. Good—I wanted to catch him off guard. I wanted him to understand I wasn't his typical financial adviser. More importantly, I realized that whatever his condition may be, his health, like the health of many retirees, would be the single greatest factor to consider when planning out his retirement strategy.

He seemed taken aback, as if nobody on my side of the desk had ever asked him this question. After a moment, he relaxed his shoulders, sat back in his chair and answered my question.

"It's MS. Diagnosed three years to this day," he finally said.

MS refers to multiple sclerosis. For those who aren't familiar, multiple sclerosis is a horrible illness where the immune system basically turns on you. It eats away at the nerves until, eventually, it affects one's ability to perform basic functions such as walking or even swallowing.

For a pre-retiree, it's a major factor to consider when calculating one's healthcare costs in retirement. It's an illness, so far, without a cure, meaning long-term care is paramount. By a certain point, when the illness became too great, David would either have to be able to afford an in-home nurse or a full-service retirement home.

"What do your financial advisers have to say about it?" I asked.

He took a moment to respond. "We haven't discussed it."

FINANCIAL PLANNING DONE RIGHT

Can you believe it?

Not one of his financial advisors had factored this most important of costs into David's retirement plan.

This is what I mean when I say there is zero consumer advocacy in the financial planning industry. This man was in a wheelchair, suffering from a disease that would eventually turn so bad, it would paralyze him. Someone would have to take care of him. David would have to either be able to afford in-home care or be able to live full time in a nursing facility, neither one of which is cheap. And neither one of his financial advisers offered him the advocacy or education he needed to factor those costs into his decision making.

I wasn't going to sit back and just let this happen to him.

So, I turned David's financial life right-side up by teaching him the art of financial self-defense.

First, I showed him what his costs are.

I punched in a few numbers: his portfolio size; a reasonable growth rate of 5 percent; annual withdrawals for expenses; and his excessive management fees.

His prognosis wasn't good.

For his $600,000 portfolio, David was going to end up paying a total of $180,000 in management fees over a period of 15 years at a growth rate of 5 percent.

The guy had no idea.

Like Richard in the last chapter, when I showed David his $600,000 portfolio was going to get sliced down to just $420,000, his jaw practically dropped to the floor.

I asked him if he was aware he was going to be charged 1.3 percent. He said no.

Then I said something that really floored him.

"Your advisor doesn't either."

He asked me how that was possible. I told him these advisors probably know all of the pros but not all the cons of the products they're pushing. They're just salespeople. It doesn't benefit them to educate you or to be your advocate. They don't care what it will end up costing you. And it doesn't benefit them to know what it is they're selling. I imagine if they knew the truth, they'd have trouble living with themselves, or at least have trouble sleeping at night.

After I showed him his costs, I showed him how he could cut them down by more than half by eliminating the internal costs. I didn't tell him which products he should invest in to achieve this. Instead, I educated him on the universe of products available to him so he could choose them for himself and I was there to guide him along the way. Then, I encouraged him to come to his own conclusions on which products made the most sense for his financial goals. It's this process of advocacy and education that is critical to the art of financial self-defense.

Needless to say, I'm happy to have David as a client to this day.

GETTING MORE FOR LESS

At this point you might be wondering: if I got David's costs down more than half, did I personally charge any fees to manage his money? Do I make *any* money on these people? How is this Jeff guy even in business?

Here's how: let's say some guy down the street offers you two pieces of bread and a slice of turkey in the middle and calls it a turkey sandwich. He wants you to pay $10 for it.

Meanwhile, across the street I offer you a turkey club with bacon, lettuce, tomato, and pickles and charge just $5.

Easy choice: you'll probably go with the turkey club.

That's basically what I do. I'm selling you a turkey club for half the cost of a plain old turkey sandwich. I charge less to offer more.

In financial terms, your typical financial advisor will end up charging you 2, 3, or 4 percent or higher in fees. That may not seem like a lot. If you have 100 percent to start and lose 4 percent, you still have 96 percent. But if your portfolio goes up 8 percent one year, and your advisor takes half, it hurts!

At my firm, Arbor Financial, we don't charge 4, 3, or even 2 percent. We charge you just 1 percent. That, or we work with a group of products that don't cost you a single thing.

Basically, we charge less than half, if that.

It may not sound like a lot. But it makes a huge difference over the life of one's portfolio. It can be the difference between hundreds of thousands and even millions of dollars.

THE RIGHT THING TO DO

Now, you might be wondering: Why do I do this? Why do I charge 1 percent or lower when many of my peers in the financial industry charge two, three, even four times that much?

It's a good question.

I could charge more but I choose not to.

I think it comes from a sense of duty that runs in the family.

I mentioned my son earlier. Like his dad, my eighteen-year-old son knew what he wanted to do with his life at an early age. At age 10 when I gave him the same talk my father gave me, my son proudly announced he was going to enter the military. Not only that, he was going to enter the Special Forces—one of the most elite members of our nation's military.

My son has always been a gifted marksman. In high school, he was a star football player, and he spent four years in the ROTC program. Recently he was accepted into a prestigious military college on a football scholarship.

And do you want to know what he did?

He declined.

Why? As my son puts it, he's saving his body for the military. It's no secret that football puts an enormous toll on the body. Statistics show that as many as 96 percent of former NFL players show signs of brain damage. My son realized that if he was going to give his all to the military, playing high-intensity college football wasn't going to work. The wear and tear on his body meant he wouldn't be able to give the U.S. military his all. It was a patriotic decision he made in service to his country.

It wasn't an easy decision, mind you. My son loves football. They were basically offering him a free ride to play it. But he realized that if he was going to be the best soldier he could possibly be, it was the right thing to do.

In my family, the right way is the only way. I bring the same philosophy to my clients.

My goal is to provide you with a radically different and *better* approach to retirement preparation than you can find anywhere else in the financial industry. I do this in service to my clients because, quite frankly, it's my job to protect them. That's what a financial adviser should do. It makes no sense that more of them don't.

Personally, I'm disgusted by the Wall Street machine that puts profit over people and the politicians who serve them. It's not easy charging 1 percent when I could easily charge twice that. I like money just as much as the next guy. But it's important to me that I do the right thing. I want my children to have a father they can be proud of.

I also recognize that there's a huge need in the market for financial advocates who work hard to educate their clients. There are enough salespeople in the world—I don't want to be one of them.

That's why I charge less to deliver more.

Not because I couldn't charge more. I could.

I do it because, like my son realized when he declined his football scholarship to save his body for the military—it's the right thing to do.

PLAYING DEFENSE

My son's high school football coaches always told his team the age old rule: the best offense is a good defense.

That's not just true in football. It's true in all aspects of life. If you're always looking ahead, you'll miss the pothole right in front of you and twist your ankle. If you've put all your money at risk, you're bound to lose it.

Let's consider the case of the 2017 Super Bowl LI between the New England Patriots and the Atlanta Falcons.

Some football fans may disagree with me on what I'm about to say. This was a very controversial game. More ink has been spilled on it than any other Super Bowl in the game's history. I promise—there's a point to this.

For those who watched it live, it was arguably the most exciting game in NFL history.

Though it didn't seem that way at the beginning.

From the start of the game, New England's offense was helpless against Atlanta's defense. They turned over the ball, could hardly make a rush, and kept digging themselves deeper and deeper into a hole. By the end of the first half, Atlanta was leading 21-3.

At halftime, everyone assumed that was the end.

I wasn't so sure.

I had been watching the New England Patriots for years. I knew the mentality of its players and of its then four-time Super Bowl Championship quarterback Tom Brady. I knew, beyond the shadow of a doubt, there was no way they'd go down during the most important game of the season without a fight. I also know what happens when people assume.

In the second half of the game, the Patriots didn't come back immediately. Four minutes into the third quarter, Atlanta managed to score another touchdown, putting them ahead 28-3. The game was as good as over.

But it wasn't. After that, it became like a different ball game.

By this point in the game, New England had learned who they were playing against. When you know your enemy, you're better able to face him. Suddenly, New England's seemingly defective defense had so exhausted the opposing team, who by this point had determined the game was all but finished, that Atlanta became powerless to stop them. As if out of nowhere, Brady played the best game of his career as he made one successful pass after another.

Suddenly, the score was 28-9.

Then, a 33-yard field goal put them up 28-12.

The odds were still against them. With five minute left on the clock, New England needed two touchdowns and two two-point conversions to tie up the game and send the two teams into overtime.

It didn't matter. It seemed as though nothing would stop the Patriots from making their historic comeback. Try as they might, the Atlanta Falcons attempted one counterattack after the next against the Patriot's formidable defense, but nearly each one of them failed. They had spent so much energy bulldozing over them for most of the game that they were unable to overpower them in those final few minutes.

Before anyone had time to breathe, the Patriots had scored another touchdown. A successful two-point conversion meant they had to do it just one more time before the clock ran out. The score was 28-20.

With just over two minutes remaining and 91 yards to go, the Patriots were bound and determined to tie up this game.

And tie it they did.

With seconds left on the clock, the Patriots scored their third touchdown of the game, followed by a second two-point conversion, to tie up the 51st Super Bowl 28-28.

By the luck of a coin toss at the beginning of the game, it was the Patriot's ball as the two teams marched into overtime. With their momentum still in play and the Falcons completely out of steam, they marched over the other team to score their fourth touchdown, closing the most exciting and controversial game in Super Bowl history 34-28.

Like I said, much ink has been spilled over what gave the Patriots their win.

The way I see it is that after the Falcons played their best hands, scoring one touchdown after another, the Patriots had the information necessary to make some critical adjustments to their defense in the second half.

However you may look at it, it was by adjusting their *defense* in the third quarter that kept the Falcons at bay, rendering them unable to score another touchdown, which gave the Patriots the room they needed to close the gap and eventually win the game.

Here's the point to all this.

If you're age 55 or above, you're like the Patriots in the third quarter of Super Bowl LI.

In the first quarter you went to college. You started your career. The score was 0-0. The possibilities were endless. The sky was the limit.

You started to make a little money. You put some or most of it into stocks and mutual funds in the second quarter—the 1990s bull market.

You made money hand over fist.

Then you got creamed.

You lost half of your money and at least a third of the equity in your home in 2000, only to have it recover and crash again in 2008. Wall Street scored one touchdown after the next against you.

Why? Because you had no defense. You were playing pure offense.

Now, it's the third quarter. You're about to enter the fourth—your retirement—and you have a decision to make.

You can keep playing the game exactly the same way you did in the first half, letting the other team's offense trample all over you.

Or you can switch your defensive strategy, hold the other team at bay, and adopt the tools and resources necessary to make up for lost time and come out ahead of the game, on your terms.

I can't pretend to know when the next bear market will hit. Anyone who says they can is kidding themselves and should probably be checked by a shrink. But I know that when the odds start to flash warning signs as they're doing today, it's best to stay prudent.

Keep a little bit of your money in the market if you enjoy the rush and the high. There's nothing wrong with that. But don't bet the house. If you do, you'll probably end up sorry at some point. It'll be like 2000 and 2008 all over again.

The market will crash again. It could happen tomorrow. It could happen 10 years from now. I don't know for certain. I have reason to believe it's coming much sooner than anyone realizes and we'll spend the next chapter discussing that.

But I have found that when you switch to a defensive, income-oriented strategy like the kind we practice at Arbor Financial, it almost doesn't matter whether the market is up, down, or all over the place. You make money and stay ahead no matter what.

Yes, it pays to be aware of the market environment. It never hurts to know when valuations are too low or too high because buying and selling opportunities can always present themselves. But when you choose not to participate in Wall Street's game, they lose power over you. That means the next time the whole thing implodes, they can't take you down with the ship. You'll already be on shore, deflating the life raft that carried you home safely.

Some people can't get enough of the game. They're like addicts.

They have dreams of unimaginable wealth that only one in 100,000 people ever achieve.

Others are unwilling to go in a separate direction from everyone else. They can't bring themselves to go left when everyone else is going right. They find peace of mind by obeying the status quo and marching to the beat of everyone else's drum.

But a few people come out different. They go against the grain. They naturally think for themselves. They zig when everyone else zags.

UNDERSTANDING FEAR

Some of my colleagues at the big financial firms I worked at earlier in my career called me crazy when I set off to work on my own. They said I'd never make it. They thought I was just scared and didn't have what it takes to play in the major leagues for keeps. They thought greed always win out over fear.

To say that, they clearly don't understand fear.

Fear comes from anxiety. Our ancestors learned to be anxious in the face of danger, so that when they came face to face with a 400-pound saber tooth tiger with razor sharp fangs almost a foot long, they could survive. Faced with that kind of danger, adrenaline would start pumping, anxiety would kick in, and if they escaped with their hide, they'd learn to *never* put themselves in that kind of situation again.

Of course, anxiety becomes a problem when it's exaggerated. Too much, and you become paralyzed by fear and the tiger gets you. Too little, you face the tiger head on and end up dead anyway. But the right amount of anxiety can help you see the danger ahead, prepare for it, and be able to respond the moment it strikes. Chances are, when you take those steps, you'll get out alive, ready to fight another day.

LIVE TO FIGHT ANOTHER DAY

We don't have to live our financial lives in a constant state of fear. If you have the right defense in place, you can avoid the kind of losses you might have suffered in 2000 and again in 2008. And, you can preserve what you've gained such that it will carry you all the way through your retirement.

You're not alone in this.

I've found many people have rightly gotten tired of the Wall Street casino, grown sick of putting their financial lives at risk, and no longer wish to put up with the headache of having huge sums of money in a market that no one can predict consistently.

That's why I'm here to tell you there's a better way.

Some of you may listen. Others may not. Not everyone will be receptive to my approach. I get it. Some people prefer the roller coaster ride to a sane and rational approach to investing. But those of you who learn to practice the art of financial self-defense will be amazed by what happens when you build your financial life on solid principles and a firm foundation.

I built my career around protecting hundreds of millions of dollars for clients who believed my way would put them ahead, and that's exactly what I've achieved.

Do you recall the case of Richard from the last chapter? Richard had $788,154 to his name when he came to see me. Following Wall Street's timeless adage of buy and hold, he could expect that number to dwindle to $234,049, a 70 percent loss of his money in 15 years. And that was a conservative estimate, assuming just a 20 percent market downturn in just one of those 15 years.

By teaching Richard the art of financial self-defense, we constructed a plan that would turn his financial life right-side up and help him make sure this outcome never occurred.

We cut his costs significantly.

We put him in safe assets that he could expect to deliver a 5 percent return each year, regardless of what happened in the broader market.

And we ensured he would never have to suffer a 20 percent loss or greater to his money, and keep his principal intact for the rest of his life, so he could pass it down to his children.

Even after calculating a $37,000 withdrawal, each year, for living expenses, Richard's principal would remain virtually unchanged.

Starting with $778,154, he could expect to still have $779,399 in 15 years.

Not $491,854 like he would have if he had stuck with Wall Street's exorbitant fees.

Not $234,049 if he had waited around for the next market crash.

Present Value: $778,154.00			Number of Years: 16			
Average Yield: 5.00%			Fees: 0.00%		Actual Yield: 5.00%	
YEAR	VAR. RATE	ANNUAL PAYMENT	COST FREE ACCT. E.O.Y.	ANNUAL MGT. FEE	NET ACCOUNT VALUE E.O.Y.	ACCOUNT DIFFERENCE
1	5.00%	-37,000	778,212		778,212	
2	5.00%	-37,000	778,272		778,272	
3	5.00%	-37,000	778,336		778,336	
4	5.00%	-37,000	778,403		778,403	
5	5.00%	-37,000	778,473		778,473	
6	5.00%	-37,000	778,546		778,546	
7	5.00%	-37,000	778,624		778,624	
8	5.00%	-37,000	778,705		778,705	
9	5.00%	-37,000	778,790		778,790	
10	5.00%	-37,000	778,880		778,880	
11	5.00%	-37,000	778,974		778,974	
12	5.00%	-37,000	779,072		779,072	
13	5.00%	-37,000	779,176		779,176	
14	5.00%	-37,000	779,285		779,285	
15	5.00%	-37,000	779,399		779,399	

Figure 7 Source: Jeff Smalls

$779,399.

That's what the art of financial self-defense looks like.

Those are the kind of results I strive to deliver for each and every one of my clients by kissing Wall Street's pro-risk, pro-growth philosophy goodbye.

We have never looked back.

And I'd bet that you won't either, if you give our way of doing things a try.

The fact of the matter is, in the fourth quarter of your life, you will actually make more spendable money by switching to a strategy that revolves around income than if you stayed in the market. At some point in the next 5, 10, or 15 years, the market will crash again. History guarantees it. If you're close to retirement, you cannot afford that kind of a hit. If you stay in the market, at some point you *will* lose money. When that happens, the only way to go is down. But if you follow the art of financial self-defense, it's much harder to go down.

3

Why You Should Get
Out of the Market

S MART ECONOMISTS NEVER try to predict the stock market. Economic theory says it's impossible. But economic theory is never perfect.

Economists assume that human beings are rational. The efficient market hypothesis suggests that stocks are priced to perfection based on rational decisions that human beings make with their money. After all, humans follow very predictable buying patterns through their lives. We spend the most on childcare products in our twenties and thirties. In our forties we spend the most on furniture. We save the most in our fifties and sixties. And we buy retirement homes, recreational vehicles, and spend the most on healthcare in our seventies and eighties.

But the world isn't that simple. If it was, and stocks moved according to predictable buying patterns, stocks would move in a straight line.

They don't.

The fact is, as much as we like to pretend that the market is rational, no one knows which direction stocks will move on any given day. If they do, they're probably doing something illegal.

Instead, stocks move according to billions and even trillions of variables that are impossible to *accurately* calculate or predict. The behavior of stocks is not rational, it's irrational—even schizophrenic.

When investors get greedy, they blow stocks out of proportion. That's what happened during the tech bubble. The same happened during the housing bubble. The same is happening again today.

But investors also spook easily. When stocks get so overpriced that they have nowhere left to go but down, they pull the plug and let the ship sink.

There's nothing "efficient" about that.

Stocks move according to the irrational decisions human beings make based on their gut feelings. Stocks follow the path of human nature. And while we can't predict stocks exactly, we can use what we understand about human nature to get pretty close.

As retirees, that's an important lesson to keep in mind.

Your broker or financial adviser will tell you stocks always go up, and they do over time. But the only emotion more powerful than greed is fear. When stocks are so expensive as they are today, there is always the risk the whole thing could come tumbling down.

I'd like to spend some time discussing this. As retirees, it's important to understand that the markets are overpriced at today's levels. Stocks can always go higher. Anything's possible. But the risk grows more severe the higher stocks climb, and stocks keep climbing higher. For every five percent you make on the upside, you risk 10 or 20 percent to the downside, maybe more.

We've just covered the importance of the art of financial self-defense. So now I'd like to take some time to survey the market to understand just how important a defensive financial strategy is to your retirement right now, based on today's prices. Let's get right to it.

WHAT'S GOOD IN THEORY...

Retiring isn't easy. That's because stocks are difficult to predict. It's easy to plan for retirement if you assume stocks always go up. Once you recognize that stocks *sometimes* go down—often for many years at a time—suddenly, it's not so simple.

Take for example a couple named Mike and Laurie.

Mike is an insurance salesman aged 60 and he and his wife have $1 million in assets to their name. They've done well so far, surviving through two brutal bear markets that left many investors in the dust. With Social Security, they figure they'll have more than enough to retire on in five years when Mike turns 65.

It sounds good in theory.

But financial planning is a whole lot more complex than that. They've failed to consider some important factors.

Namely, what if the market goes through another tailspin like in 2000 and 2008? History supports the idea that a 20 percent drop is inevitable sooner or later. Bear markets happen, on average, once every four years. The current bull market has lasted for eight. At some point, a 20 percent drop is practically guaranteed. But what if it's worse? And what if it comes sooner, not later?

If it's as bad as last time, and Mike keeps his diversified portfolio of stocks and stock mutual funds, he could be looking at another 50 percent drop that leaves him with just $500,000 in assets, half of what he had before.

Under those circumstances, he may have to delay retirement, and even once he's able to retire, there's no telling if he'll be able to maintain his lifestyle once he does. He may have to downsize his home, give up on ideas of traveling the globe, and be unable to leave as much to his family.

It might happen. It might not.

Fortunately, we don't need to concern ourselves with what *will* happen.

What we do need to concern ourselves with is the *chance* or even the probability that something could go wrong, not whether or not it actually does. With stocks as high as they are today, that's an easy bet to make. You might miss out on a few more gains. But who wants to bet a dollar for the chance to earn five cents?

If there's a chance you could lose half of your money tomorrow, wouldn't you want to have a financial safety net in place? A defensive strategy that helps you avoid the carnage once it hits?

Think back to what it felt like during the last two bear markets.

Now imagine going through that again.

I'm here to tell you that the chances of it happening again are much higher than anyone is willing to think. And I want to help you avoid it once it happens.

FOR EVERY ACTION...

Bear markets happen. It's a fact of life. Newton's third law states that for every action there's an equal and opposite reaction. It all comes back to gravity: what goes up must come down. You're buying a new dress for your wife at Saks Fifth Avenue one minute, and shopping in the clearance aisle at Macy's the next.

Life can always throw you a curveball. When my wife and I were told our newborn daughter would never be able to see, it crushed us. Our precious child who we brought into the world would never have a normal life—instead, it would be a hard and difficult one.

Fortunately, that wasn't the case. Our daughter can now see. Not only that, she's excelling in every area. We suffered a small downturn when the experts were predicting a full-blown bear market. It could've been much worse.

For the sake of everyone, I hope the next downturn isn't a bad one. I hope it won't be as bad as I believe it will be.

But I've been in this industry far too long and I've seen too much to *honestly* believe that's the case.

Everything I've studied points to the fact that the next downturn will be a bad one. Some of my research indicates it could be even worse than the last two. That's all the more reason to adjust your financial strategy to a defensive one as you head into retirement.

HISTORY ALWAYS REPEATS ITSELF

In 1999, months before the tech bubble burst, my warning signs went off. I knew it was time to get out of the market. Unfortunately, I couldn't do anything to protect my clients. This was back when I worked for one of the big financial firms. The higher ups told us to keep peddling product. The market was hot. Everything was a buy. If I had warned my clients that the bubble was ready to pop, it would've been a black mark on my career I would've carried to this day. So, I was forced to watch as my clients suffered through the worst downturn in a quarter century, offering them reassuring advice that the market would someday return to its previous levels. Instead of carrying a black mark on my career, I carried one on my conscience. Fortunately, stocks returned to those previous levels in 2007. But we all know what happened next.

You may recall the end of the 1993 Oscar-winning film *Schindler's List*. It's one of Steven Spielberg's finest films and probably the best performance of Liam Neeson's career.

Oskar Schindler, the film's protagonist, arrives in Krakow, Poland to staff a factory dedicated to manufacturing weapons at the start of World War II. As the Nazis begin exterminating Jews, Schindler persuades his Nazi superiors to leave the Jews who work at his factories alone so they could continue producing weapons. His superiors agree, and soon after, Schindler begins requesting additional Jewish labor to rescue as many of them from the extermination camps as he can.

To avoid detection, Schindler leaves a few lines blank at the bottom of his labor request forms. Had he filled it to the bottom of the page, the Nazis might have suspected him for harboring Jews for safety. In one of the most heartbreaking scenes toward the end of the film, Oskar reflects on how he could have saved even just one additional life had he not selfishly chosen to protect his own skin by leaving that one line blank. Had he done more, he could have saved many more lives.

I don't pretend to be saving anyone's life. But as a financial adviser, it's my job to help clients protect their livelihood, which is almost as, if not equally, important. To this day I regret not choosing to brush off my superiors in the 2000 tech bubble and tell my clients to protect themselves. That's why I went independent soon after, and by the time the 2007 meltdown came around, I was able to see the warning signs a mile away and rush dozens of clients to safety.

Now, I'm looking at another meltdown and I believe it's coming faster than anyone realizes. All of our clients are prepared for the worst. But I realize my job is never done. It's never done so long as there are people still being duped by the Wall Street machine that tells them to buy whenever the market's hot. It will turn on them when they least expect it.

I wish I had been able to help my clients in 2000. I wish I had been able to help more in 2008. This time, I hope to get this message out to anyone willing to read it so no one will have to go through one of those horrifying events again.

WHAT BULL MARKETS LOOK LIKE, AND WHY THIS ONE IS LOSING STEAM

Let's review some of the reasons why now is the optimum time to prepare your financial strategy for a bear market scenario.

Since the year 1900, the stock market has fallen into a bear market twenty-five times, or on average once every 4.4 years. The current bull market, which began in March 2009, is pushing on nine years—twice the length of the average bull market.

There's a possibility the current bull market will be like the long 1982–1999 bull market that lasted for seventeen years and saw the Dow gain over ten times its value. But I find that to be unlikely.

That bull market paved the way for new and innovative technologies that changed the way we live forever. It saw the rise of the personal computer and the Internet, two technologies that are still in use today.

Think of how much the Internet has transformed our lives. Email revolutionized the way we communicate. For the first time in human history, a written message that once took days or even weeks to send could now be sent in a matter of seconds. Google Web search has revolutionized our productivity, allowing us to access the world's information from our fingertips, also in seconds, and it has disrupted traditional businesses such as newspapers, travel agencies, music, telecommunications, and many other industries.

Certain estimates put the value of the Internet in 2014 at about $966 billion or 6 percent of GDP at that time.

Can you think of any technology emerging today that will be anywhere near as big?

I can't.

Artificial intelligence is still a long way off.

Virtual reality is struggling to even take off within a large population.

Precision medicine, while exciting, will take years and even decades to fully disrupt the healthcare industry.

Electric cars are years and even decades away from carving out a significant niche in their market.

Some who are more optimistic may say big technological breakthroughs such as these are coming faster than anyone thinks. Technology moves exponentially. Still, I don't think these people appreciate just how long it takes for breakthrough technologies to go mainstream.

Today, everyone and their grandmother has a cellular phone, most likely its more advanced version, the smartphone. Smartphones are incredibly advanced pieces of technology that essentially put the power of a computer in the palm of your hand.

But few stop to realize how far the smartphone and its predecessor, the cell phone, have come.

The first mobile phones arrived all the way back in the mid-1940s. They weren't even that mobile; they were attached to the inside of your car.

Fast forward into the mid-1980s and cell phones were big, bulky pieces of plastic with huge antennas that were little more than an advanced walkie-talkie. Many cost as much as $4,000 dollars for an entry level phone. The businessman was the only true market for this enormous device.

It wasn't until the late 1990s that cell phones grew affordable enough to carve their way into a large consumer market. And it wasn't until the turn of the last decade that smartphones fully saturated the market. All in all, that's around fifty-five years of evolution from start to finish.

Or take for instance the personal computer. The first computers were invented all the way back during World War II and were used to hack Nazi encryptions. They were as large as a small house.

In 1957, IBM shipped the first hard drive for people to store files and data and sold them for as much as $10,000 per megabyte. Today you can buy a computer with 64 gigabytes, each of which carries 1,000 megabytes, and get it for $500. Plus, these items were as big as a refrigerator. The first truly personal computers didn't arrive on the scene until the late 1970s and didn't fully saturate the market until 20 years later in the mid-to-late 1990s.

Look throughout history and you'll find that every major innovation took years before everyone used them. The light bulb. The steam engine. The printing press. All the way to the technologies of today like the Internet, the personal computer, and the smartphone.

That's why I believe that people who are banking on a major technological innovation that will carry the market forward are kidding themselves.

Across the economy, you'll find that most major industries have peaked. When industries peak, a crash shortly follows.

The auto industry is just one example. The stock prices of nearly every leading automaker are all fully entrenched in their own bear market. Just look at the "Big Three" U.S. auto makers. Ford stock is well off its recent highs. Fiat Chrysler is struggling to make new highs. And General Motors has been flat lining for several years. Not only are investors looking to the future of electric and automated vehicles—which has driven companies like Volvo to plan to fully electrify their cars within the next couple of years—but auto sales are also sharply down. Auto sales are down as much as 7 percent from a year ago. That's a multibillion dollar hit to the industry's budget.

The retail industry is also slumping. Close to 6,300 stores closed in just over the first half of 2017. U.S. retailers are actually on pace to close more stores in 2017 than during the Great Recession in 2008. Not only that, more than 300 retailers have filed for bankruptcy so far this year, a 31 percent increase from a year prior.

And it's not middle income consumer destinations that are the only ones struggling to keep up. Luxury retailers are floundering too: companies like Coach, Tiffany, Ralph Lauren, and many others are struggling to prop up sales. Luxury retailer Michael Kors is closing more than 100 of its stores. And with the fall of the retail industry, so comes the fall of the American mall. Most high-end malls will probably remain okay. But it's the middle America malls, anchored by stores like J.C. Penney and Sears, that might be forced to close shop. Those anchor stores are where malls get most of their business. You've likely heard Sears is in danger of going bankrupt. There was a lot of speculation about it this year. Rather than file for bankruptcy, the company decided to close 300 more of its stores, despite already closing hundreds in years prior. That likely means the beginning of the end for 300 different malls. J.C. Penney is also closing 138 of its stores. And Macy's is closing sixty-eight.

FIG. 8. **Store Closures 2000 to 2017**

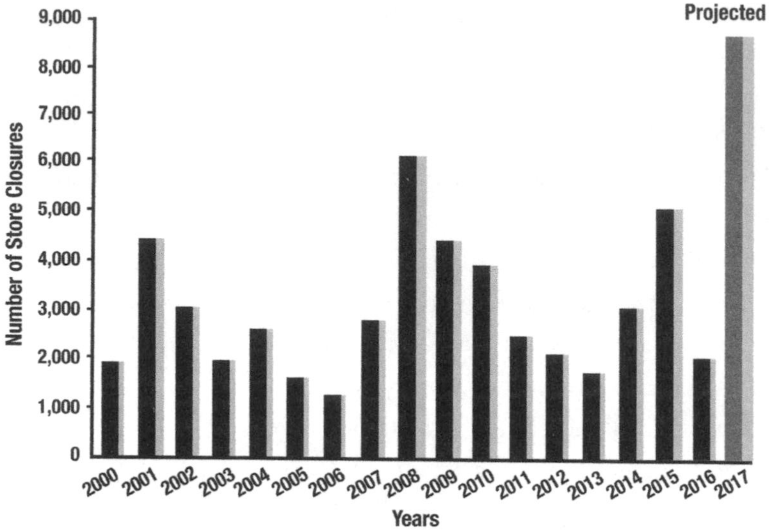

Source: https://www.theatlas.com/charts/HJRt55iCg

This trend grows worse the deeper you look. Not only are people more wary about buying consumer goods, they're not even having as many children. The U.S. birth rate fell 8 percent during the Great Recession and never recovered.[1] Birth rates have continued to plummet to record lows. With fewer babies comes a whole host of consumer markets that will take a hit. Baby food, toys, clothes, and diapers. But beyond that, fewer children means fewer workers to help prop up the economy in the future. With fewer workers comes a weaker economy.

We're already seeing a decline in income levels across the board. Adjusted for inflation, real incomes are 12.4 percent lower than they were at the peak of the tech bubble in 1999. They're even 5 percent lower than the 1970s! Meanwhile, the bottom 90 percent of people have seen their share of the overall income drop from 68 percent in 1975 to just 49 percent today, while the top 0.1 percent of people have seen their income levels rise *four times*. Not only that, today more than half of Americans have less than $1,000 in savings.[2]

This is not a strong economy. Without a vibrant middle class, our economy can never hope to improve. And without a strong economy, stocks can never hope to stay this high.

I don't mean to preach doom and gloom. There are plenty of people for that. I merely invite you to take a closer look at the economic reality facing us today and ask yourself: if you're close to retirement, do you really think the stock market will continue to go up over the next 5, 10, or 15 years given the weakness we're seeing across the economy? Or does it make sense to hunker down, go on defense, and wait for the upcoming storm to blow over?

The only unknown that might send the economy racing higher, besides an unanticipated bear market, would be some new disruptive technology on the horizon. If it were my retirement, I wouldn't bank on it.

THE DEMOGRAPHIC PROBLEM

There are plenty of other reasons to believe the stock market is teetering on the edge of another major downturn. I'll just go into a couple more of them.

I mentioned earlier that U.S. birth rates are slowing down to record lows. There's actually a much bigger story there that affects us right now.

Everyone loves to take a dig at millennials. They're too lazy. They're entitled. They spend too much time on their phones. Personally, I give millennials credit for being some of the most tech-savvy people on the planet. But there is one indisputable fact I can say about them.

They aren't having as many children.

This is understandable for a variety of reasons.

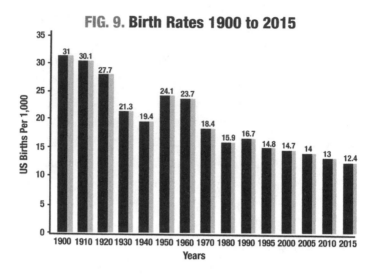

FIG. 9. **Birth Rates 1900 to 2015**

Source: U.S. Census CDC

As child rearing has grown more expensive, young parents have put their focus on raising just one or two children. Even most baby boomers, who came from families of five, seven or even ten children chose to have just two or three.

This has happened for a couple of reasons. As inflation has carried our economy forward, it has also made the costs of goods and services more expensive.

Take for instance the cost of childcare.

Childcare costs have risen to obscene levels over the past decade. It's gotten so bad that many working mothers are opting to stay home rather than give over a quarter of her or her husband's take-home pay to babysitters.

Then there's college tuition. College tuition for all intents and purposes is in bubble territory. From 1980 to 2010, the cost of college tripled from $9,800 to $27,300. More premium institutions charge upward of $40,000 to $50,000 per year.[3] No one but the top few percent of Americans can afford to send their children to these elite institutions without financial assistance. Many American parents are forced to tell their children that unless they want to go into debt or somehow put themselves through college, they're out of luck. With tuition prices so high, who can blame them?

But beyond all that, kids are just plain expensive. You have to buy diapers—tons and tons of them. You have to buy several sets of over-priced clothes as they grow out of them with each passing month. It's an additional mouth to feed. You have to buy them furniture, invest in hobbies like sports or music. The list goes on and on.

It's never been easy to raise a child, but nowadays it's even harder. To raise a child born today, it will cost parents over $250,000 from the time the child is born to the time they leave home. A quarter million bucks just for following nature's course. The average American who has less than $1,000 in the bank, quite frankly, can't afford that. Not by a long shot.

Fortunately, we're still having children. But it's completely under-standable why we're not having as many.

FEWER KIDS MEANS FEWER WORKERS

Ultimately, there's an economic side to this.

The baby boomers had the benefit of immense population growth that carried the economy higher. Not only were there more workers, but as women began entering the workforce in large numbers, labor forces grew even higher.

Not only that, but the baby boomers saw a massive surge in attend-ing higher education. So not only were there more workers, there were more educated workers.

All of this goes to explain why the economy grew so enormously during the 1980s and 1990s bull market that saw baby boomers enter the labor force.

And it also goes to explain why the economy has been so stagnant for so many years.

The baby boomers didn't have as many children as their parents did. Less children means fewer workers.

The economy is also "used" to college-educated workers. That's why you see so many millennials today struggling to get decent entry-level jobs after they've graduated. The economic benefit of college just isn't what it used to be back when college was first being widely attended.

And as I mentioned before, there are no emerging technologies of great social and economic significance, such as electricity and the Internet, that are primed to take the economy to new, unprecedented levels.

But there's a larger issue at play as well.

As the baby boomers are now entering their retirement years, there aren't enough millennial workers to replace them. Mind you, there are actually more millennials than there are baby boomers. But the baby boomers were born so rapidly over such a small period of time, that as they retire, many economists fear they'll take the economy down with it. Said another way, they'll retire faster than the economy can keep up. Even if it can supply new workers, it's a question of whether those workers will have as much spending power. If you think of it in terms of the waves in the ocean, the millennials are like a 10-foot wave. They're a force to be reckoned with. But the baby boomers are a 30 footer.

That means that as the baby boomers continue to retire, they'll have less and less room for discretionary spending. For example, think about where you are in your life. Hopefully the kids have all moved out of the house and are starting their careers. You may be at the peak of your career, throwing thousands if not tens of thousands into your savings and retirement, hoping that by the time the clock strikes 65 or 66, you'll have enough retirement funds to call it quits.

It might be good for *you* to be saving all that money. But it's bad for the economy. Less spending means less money goes to someone else. That's less money for the grocer, the retailer, the lawyer, the banker— anyone who might have once relied on you for your business.

I'm not saying you should go out and spend more money for the good of the people. This whole book is about making sure you're putting enough away for retirement to be able to enjoy it.

What I am saying is the simple economic reality of what happens when large swaths of people funnel into retirement. If it happens too fast, and too quickly, it's an economic recipe for disaster.

A GLOBAL PHENOMENON

This isn't just America's fate. This is the fate of every major developed country across the entire world.

Think about it this way.

What would you rather invest in? A small, innovative company that costs $10 per share or a large, multinational corporation that costs $300 per share?

At first, you might think the larger company. It's a household name, it's been in business for years and it's been a reliable stock for years.

The $10 stock, however, has survived the startup phase, has plenty of cash on its balance sheet, has little in the way of debt, and is carving out a significant portion of its market. The large, multinational corporation, meanwhile, that has already peaked, is already a household name, and is struggling to find new business elsewhere. And instead of charging $10 a share with room to climb higher, they charge $300 a share with more room for it to go down.

It's an easy choice.

The larger, $300-a-share company might be bigger and badder, but they won't give investors as much bang for their buck.

The smaller, $10-a-share company, however, has plenty of room to run higher and could potentially reward investors with a 10-times return on their money or more if things go according to plan.

America, and most developed countries, are in a similar position.

They've already advanced to first-world status. Their economies have already climbed exponentially higher from their origins. Sure, they can always climb higher. But the rate of growth will never be what it was, say, during the 1980s and 1990s economic boom in the United States that saw the greatest period of social and economic advancement arguably in world history. And today, its middle class is beginning to collapse.

Japan is perhaps the best example of any developed country in this situation.

You may be at least somewhat familiar with the situation over there. Japan has what some market analysts call a "demographic time bomb." Over the last five years, the country has watched $2 trillion disappear from its annual GDP and seen the population drop by one million. Two trillion might sound bad, but a million people sounds like a drop in the bucket considering Japan has a population of nearly 127 million people.

But one million people is a lot when you think about it, considering the trend looks much, much worse.

While Japan has roughly 127 million people today, its population is expected to plummet to just 88 million by 2065, dropping further to 51 million by 2115.

So, in the next 50 years, Japan's population will shrink by a third.

In another 50 years, it will drop by more than half.

Then there's the makeup of its citizens. Today, a quarter of its population, or 25 percent, is over the age of 65. By 2065, that figure will rise to nearly half.

I realize I just threw a lot of numbers at you, so I'll put it in simple terms.

Japan is dying.

As its population continues to age and shrink, with death rates well overshadowing its birth rates, Japan's economy will slowly but surely fade from existence.

FIRST WORLD PROBLEMS

How did this happen?

For one, the Japanese seem to be completely disinterested in populating the country.

Then there's the other factor: they simply can't afford children in the first place. And this is where it gets scary, because America has the same problem.

Japanese wages have stagnated since the 1990s. This is back when everyone thought the Japanese economy was going to become the largest in the world and eventually buy out U.S. businesses. That didn't happen. Instead, Japan went through the worst economic crash in its nation's history, falling in and out of recession for the better part of the last 30 years. Over that time, Japan's GDP has increased on average by just 1.3 percent per year, nearly half that of the United States—a truly abysmal figure.

But this isn't just Japan's fate.

This is the fate of every developed nation in the world today.

Great Britain, Germany, the United States—all of us are vulnerable to the very plague that has washed over Japan.

Decades of low birth rates in the developed world have slowed the flow of young people into the workforce. Today the U.S. birth rate is roughly 1.8, meaning that every woman of child-bearing age has 1.8 kids on average. Obviously nobody can have 1.8 children, but it means that for every four mothers that have two children there is one mother who only has one.

Unfortunately, 1.8 is too low.

Developed countries such as the United States need to have a birth rate of 2.1 births per woman in order to sustain population. Granted, we're in much better shape than Japan, which has a birth rate of just 1.4—50 percent less than it needs to be—and even Germany with a birth rate of 1.5. These countries will face major demographic challenges in the years ahead due to their paltry birth rates.

At the same time, the baby boomer generation is retiring in droves. To get an idea of the scale, 10,000 boomers retire *each day*.

That may sound hard to believe. If 10,000 baby boomers retire each day, and there are 365 days in a year, that means that approximately 3.65 million boomers retire each year. It sounds impossible, but it's true. These figures are confirmed by such organizations as the Social Security Administration and Pew Research. A 2010 report from Pew Research states, "On January 1, 2011, the oldest baby boomers will turn 65. Every day for the next 19 years, about 10,000 more will cross that threshold. By 2030, when all the baby boomers will have turned 65, fully 18 percent of the nation's population will be at least that age."

So we have a situation where low birth rates mean fewer people entering the workforce, while an aging generation of baby boomers are retiring and therefore exiting the workforce.

Not only that, since these retirees are largely cutting down costs— save perhaps medical expenses—they are no longer spending enough to buff up the economy.

The U.S. Census Bureau estimates that by 2030, the number of working-age people available to support each retiree will fall from just over five today, to barely three. Hence, America's population is aging, growing more dependent, and less able to provide for itself.

This is the very same fate that has plagued Japan for the last 30 years, and look what happened to them.

I don't think our own fate will be anywhere near as bad as Japan's.

We have nearly three times their population, our economy is more robust and diverse, and America quite frankly is still the most powerful country in the world. However, we're heading in the same direction. We are Japan on a 10-to-15 year lag. That means if you are age 65 today and hoping your retirement funds will still be around to support you by the time you turn 75 or 80, you need to pay close attention.

Long term, Japan's stock market has been a dead man walking.

Overtime, as investors realize America will suffer the same or similar fate, investors will dump U.S. equities and flee to more prosperous economies that are still on the rise such as India and maybe China (though I wouldn't bet on that last one—India is a much better bet and growing at a more sustainable rate than China ever did).

Is it possible we could have another baby boom in the near future? Of course. Anything's possible. But a few things would have to happen in order for that to occur:

1. **Childcare rates would have to fall.** In order to keep more women in the workforce, women will have to demand their employers either offset childcare expenses or supply childcare services themselves. This is a double-edged sword. More workers mean more spenders and more spenders mean a stronger economy. But save regulations that combat discrimination, employers will be less likely to hire a worker that comes attached with expected entitlement benefits than they will with someone who doesn't. Either way, something will have to be done. Statistics show that 20 percent of working parents spent a quarter of their take-home pay on childcare, and in 33 states and the District of Columbia, childcare services cost more than public college tuition.[4] This is a crisis with devastating social and economic consequences that will have to be solved in order for parents to feel comfortable raising more kids.

2. **The college tuition bubble will have to pop.** Today's high school curriculums are designed to give students the tools they need to be college-ready by the time they graduate. We can debate how well schools are doing that, but the fact remains that today's economy almost requires students to have a college degree. It is almost expected, and even then, many jobs are now requiring a master or even a doctorate-level degree. Unless you're a skillful and business-savvy entrepreneur with remarkable interpersonal and social skills, you need at least a college degree to survive on your own in the economy. That means, anytime a parent has a child, they're carrying a millstone around their head of $68,524—the average cost to send a child to college for four years at a lower-end school, or as much as $154,356 or more for a higher-end one.[5] That is no minor expense, and it's one all parents have in the back of their mind when they consider having more kids.

3. **Increased subsidies for child-rearing parents.** Save a cut to childcare expenses and college tuition costs, the federal government would have to increase the subsidies and tax breaks it offers to new parents in order to encourage people to have more children. Unfortunately, with our government more than $20 trillion in debt, that scenario seems unlikely, though it wouldn't be the first time the government spent money it didn't have.

4. **The economy will have to improve.** This is the big one. Since the Great Recession birth rates have declined, not because people didn't want kids, but because they think they can't afford them. Today's generation of young people are all too aware of the devastating consequences of the 2000 tech bust and the 2008 financial crisis. It caused arguments in the home and strife in the family. After experiencing that trauma, they are less likely to purchase a home, less likely to buy equities, and less likely to commit to a career if they think it might be under threat by automation or other economic circumstances. Fact is, they watched their par-

ents suffer through the two worst market failures in generations and they're desperate to avoid the same fate. They're scared, and scared people don't spend money. They save it, they hoard it, or they become so plagued by the fear of failure that they never figure out how to make it (you likely know a young person like that yourself). Not to mention, with more than $1 trillion dollars in student debt on their shoulders, many of our most productive young workers will spend the majority of their professional lives paying down debts rather than contributing to the greater economy. This hurts all of us.

In other words, several hurdles are standing in the way of another massive baby boom that would take the economy to new levels.

Even then, if a baby boom were to happen, we wouldn't feel the economic benefits of it right away.

Childcare-related industries would soon benefit, but the wider economy wouldn't enjoy this new influx of people until these children reach employable age, supplying additional souls to the labor force and increasing productivity across the nation.

China is in a similar situation. Having recently repealed their decades-old one-child policy in which they limited married individuals from having multiple children to keep their population growth in check, the Chinese will have to wait an entire generation before they feel the economic benefits of having more kids.

WHAT'S PROPPING UP THE MARKET

These are the headwinds we face as retirees and pre-retirees today. Demographic constraints will ultimately hinder the economy over the coming years as the number of millennials entering the workforce fails to keep up with the number of baby boomers who are retiring. Not only that, but most major U.S. industries have either peaked or are entering decline. The automotive, retail, and oil and natural gas industries have come under severe pressure in recent years while technological firms that promise increased automation (and therefore a loss of human jobs) are on the up and up.

You can see this in companies' financials over the past several years. As most major businesses have peaked, companies have resorted to "financial engineering" in order to inflate their stock prices. Financial engineering sounds illegal, but most of it actually isn't. The most well-known example has been the use of corporate buybacks.

Here's how it works. Management teams have two primary goals: grow the business and raise their stock prices. Doing one will achieve the other, but not the other way around. If business is booming, the stock will likely increase in value. But there are other ways to improve a stock's price if business is also slipping. That's where we are today as most industries have reached their peak, but management teams have been incentivized to raise their stock prices.

Essentially, as revenues and earnings have continued to slip, companies have taken on new debt in order to fund repurchases of their own stock in order to keep stock prices higher.

HOW BUYBACKS WORK

Here's an example. Let's say a publicly traded company releases a certain number of shares into the market. Let's say the company has a market cap of $10 billion, meaning that's how much the company is worth. The company has one billion shares valued at $10 each for a total of $10 billion, the company's value.

If investor A owns one million shares of the company's stock, he has $10 million worth of shares.

FIG. 10.
How Buybacks Boost Earnings Per Share (EPS)

	Pre-Buyback	Earnings Per Share
Earnings	$1,000,000	
Shares Outstanding	1,000,000	= $1.00

	Post-Buyback (40,000 Shares)	
Earnings	$1,000,000	
Shares Outstanding	960,000	= $1.04

Source: https://www.finra.org/investors/how-companies-use-their-cash-buyback

If investor B has one thousand shares, his total value is $10,000. Pretty simple.

Now, let's say our public company has recently come under pressure due to a competitor that has inserted itself into the marketplace. Wall Street analysts have projected the stock to slip—nothing major, but even a 5 to 10 percent correction of a company's stock can get a CEO fired. So, rather than invest in the business to fight back against its competitors, or other headwinds to the business such as a drop in demand, the company will choose to buy back shares of its own stock in order to inflate the value of the remaining shares. This will keep investors happy and corporate executives in a job.

Here's what that looks like. Let's say out of the company's billion shares, two hundred million, or 20 percent, are available in the open market, meaning these shares haven't been purchased. The other 80 percent are owned by individual investors, corporate institutions, or insiders at the company itself.

Out of the two hundred million shares available, the company decides to repurchase four hundred thousand of those shares, or one-fifth of the shares remaining. Since each share costs $10, it will cost the company $400 million to make the purchase. The company doesn't have any money in the bank, so they decide to purchase the shares on margin, which is a fancy way of saying they borrow money to buy the shares. In other words, they go into debt to make themselves *seem* better than they're actually doing.

If you're thinking that's a terrible use of a company's money, you're right.

But this is where it gets interesting.

The company's market cap or value hasn't changed. It's still worth $10 billion. Before, each of the billion shares was worth $10. However, with only 960 million shares remaining, each share is now worth approximately $10.40 instead of $10.00, meaning each share got roughly a four percent bump. That's because each share now holds more of the company's value than it did before.

Investors are happy because their stocks just went up 4 percent.

Corporate executives and members of the board are happy because insiders aren't screaming at them to be fired. Many of them also own company stock, so they've benefited as well, and many more receive additional compensation anytime the company's stock goes up.

Never mind the fact the company went into debt to make this all happen. Ultimately, all Wall Street cares about is whether they get paid—whether that money comes from you or whether they make it appear out of thin air. Either way, they got paid. It may be a short-term solution to a long-term problem, but greed has never been useful for long-term planning, strategy is—a lesson retirees and pre-retirees should well heed.

A CANCER IN THE MARKET

This is where it gets ugly. Corporations aren't just digging themselves into a hole. They're digging a hole for everyone.

Case in point, a large portion of the market's gains we've seen since the market bottomed in March 2009 following the Great Recession were thanks to these corporate buybacks.

A team of market analysts at Goldman Sachs, led by chief U.S. equity strategist David Kostin, reports that "corporate repurchases [or share buybacks] are the main source of net demand for U.S. stocks." They found that share buybacks accounted for 46.6 percent of purchases in the first quarter of 2017. In other words, nearly half of stocks were purchased not because the market demanded it, but because companies are desperate to keep the gravy train rolling. A report from analysts at HSBC bank agrees that the majority of the demand for U.S. stocks has come from share buybacks.

Let that sink in for a second. The primary demand for U.S. stocks—the single greatest factor that has kept the market rising higher and higher since 2009—has nothing to do with the market's demand for equities, but rather companies who concocted a way to essentially "rig" the system, repurchasing their own shares in an effort to bid the market ever higher. The last time we saw a major market force rig the system, we saw 40-year-old stay-at-home mothers without a penny to their names buying houses on leverage and flipping them during the housing bubble thanks to stupid policies that allowed such practices. And we all know how that ended.

But here's where you should be wary. Buybacks have started to slump. Once they really start to crater, as interest rates rise, it could very well provide the market with its next tipping point.

Buybacks peaked in 2015 at $572.2 billion, a 3.1 percent increase from the year prior, after increasing nearly every year all the way back to 2009. In 2016, buybacks for the year slowed to $536.4 billion, a 6.3

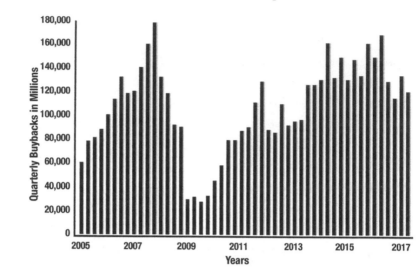

FIG. 11. S&P 500 Quarterly Share Purchases

Source: Data from www.factset.com/data/news

percent decrease from the fiscal year 2015. And 2017 is looking to be on pace for another steep decline. In the first quarter of 2017, stock buybacks fell 17.5 percent from the first quarter a year prior to $133.1 billion.

You'll notice that buybacks haven't quite reached the peak they hit in 2007 before the market entered a tailspin. But the fact that corporate buybacks are beginning to deteriorate should scare even the most optimistic investor, considering they've been one of the primary sources of demand for U.S. equities since the financial crisis.

This is yet another example of how Wall Street does not have your best interests in mind. They tell you to keep buying equities because they always go up. It creates a self-fulfilling prophecy whereby investors plow into the market, unaware of the forces actually bidding the market higher. When the carpet gets pulled out from under them and the buybacks dry up, it won't be institutional investors that feel the most pain. It will be the mom and pop investors who think this time will be different. The reality is, the system's been rigged. When the buybacks stop, I believe the whole market will come crashing down.

If you really want to get a sense for how much your financial adviser has your best interests at heart, ask him: "What do you think about the slump in corporate buybacks?"

See what he or she says. If it sounds like funny-money talk, walk away immediately. Take your money with you.

QE, THE FED, AND DEFLATION

The question you might be wondering is—where did these companies get all the money to make these ridiculous purchases?

You can thank our own U.S. government for that.

Whereas corporations used share buybacks to push their stock prices up, the government was conducting its own financial engineering deep in the heart of the Federal Reserve System, the institution of unelected officials responsible for managing the country's monetary policy.

You have probably heard the phrase "quantitative easing," or QE, passed around a few times on the Internet or the cable news channels in recent years.

QE was a system designed by the Federal Reserve to pump money into the economy after the Great Recession.

Central banks, like our own Federal Reserve, or the European Central Bank and the Bank of Japan, are given the challenge of keeping inflation in check. Too much inflation and the economy overheats—goods are too expensive. This is what happened in the 1970s hyperinflation. Too little, on the other hand, and the economy freezes—demand slows down as people stop buying. This is what happened in the 1930s Great Depression.

Whereas the 1970s were characterized by a period of "hyperinflation," the 1930s was a period of "deflation," the opposite of inflation or hyperinflation. Deflation is a scary thing. It basically means the economy is dying. This is the same force that caused the economy to slow down during the financial crisis. Central banks like the Federal Reserve aim to curb deflation by shooting for what some call the "Goldilocks Zone"—a point at which inflation is neither too hot nor too cold. Too hot and the economy grows too quickly, leaving some behind. Too cold and the economy dies, putting people out of work. So, the Federal Reserve shoots for minor inflation. They judge that to be an economic growth rate of 2 percent. However, the U.S. economy has struggled to keep, let alone maintain, that level throughout the recovery.

HOW THE FED RIGGED THE ECONOMY

So, how does the Fed shoot for that 2 percent goal?

Before the financial crisis, central banks managed inflation by adjusting the overnight interest rate, or the rate at which banks lend each other overnight. This is called the fed funds rate, or the benchmark interest rate that determines and sets other interest rates.

Essentially, if companies were unsure about the future of the economy and started to cut back on investment, the Federal Reserve would reduce the overnight rate. This, in theory, would encourage businesses to borrow money from banks. The idea was that this would reduce the bank's funding costs and encourage them to make more loans and keep the economy from falling into recession.

On the flip side, if inflation was starting to get out of hand, and people and businesses were buying goods on credit like there's no tomorrow, the Federal Reserve would raise the fed funds rate to make loans more expensive, and discourage businesses and investors from borrowing.

When the Great Recession hit, the Federal Reserve slashed the fed funds rate as far as it could go, almost to zero, an unprecedented and astonishing move that was meant to boost the economy. In theory, this would encourage businesses to borrow as much money as they possibly could.

Suddenly, money was cheap. Money was so cheap they could borrow as much as they wanted for such little interest that if it produced any ROI, it was essentially free. Think about it: free money! This additional influx of cash would thereby boost business, flow into the economy, and make everyone happy. Or so they thought.

Fact is, it didn't work.

Despite slashing the fed funds rate to zero, the arbiters of our nation's monetary policy were unable to spark a recovery.

So, they brought out the big guns.

THE BIGGEST AND MOST UNTESTED EXPERIMENT IN MONETARY POLICY HISTORY

Our nation's central bank began experimenting with a new form of monetary policy—written about in textbooks, but never actually tested out in the economy. They called it quantitative easing, or "QE."

Basically how this works is, central banks all over the world began to "create money" by buying securities, like government bonds, back from banks. Now, banks had more money to lend out to creditors, individuals, and businesses. Essentially, it was like printing money out of thin air, since the money didn't exist to begin with. In a way, it's cheating. But this is the government we're talking about. The government can do whatever it wants. It doesn't matter whether or not it makes sense, is proven to work, or whether it does more harm than it does good.

In the Fed's case, they bought back government bonds from the U.S. Treasury and other banks, similar to how corporations repurchased their own stock. This was supposed to give banks additional cash to either lend out to creditors or buy new assets. The idea was that by making it easier to obtain loans, interest rates would drop, and consumers and businesses would borrow lots of money. Once borrowed, they would go out into the economy and spend.

Theoretically, more spending means more consumption. More consumption leads to greater demand for goods and services. Greater demand leads to more jobs to meet demand. And more jobs means a stronger economy.

The question is, did it work?

We'll get to that in a minute.

But to get an idea of just how much the Federal Reserve has relied on this policy since the Great Recession, the size of its balance sheet—meaning the amount it has borrowed from banks in order to stimulate the economy—has grown from $1 trillion in 2007, a staggering figure in its own right, to more than $4 trillion today, a mind-boggling 300 percent increase.

In other words, the Fed made a $3 trillion bet on this program.

You'd think it would work, right?

MISSION FAILURE

So, did it?

You tell me.

Do you feel confident enough to go out and borrow a bunch of money and spend it like there's no tomorrow for the "economic good?"

In theory, a policy as ambitious as QE is supposed to signal to the economy and markets that the Federal Reserve is serious about propping up the economy, fighting deflation, lowering unemployment, and raising consumer confidence.

What they failed to consider is that it might do just the opposite, which is exactly what happened.

Rather than encourage consumers to borrow and spend, Americans and consumers all over the world were so jolted by the financial crisis that they refused to take on any additional debt by taking out loans. The fact that the Fed and other central banks made money essentially "free" didn't help either. If anything, they played their hand too strong. They were too eager. It's the age-old principle that if a thing looks too good to be true, it probably is. And if "free money" isn't too good to be true, I don't know what is.

The irony here is that in their attempt to bolster the economy by increasing confidence, the Federal Reserve—at least in my mind—actually *lowered* confidence, by engineering such a ridiculous concept as "free money," throwing it around the economy to try to get people to spend, thereby spooking people who understood that this was far from normal.

In other words, it made them look desperate.

People aren't stupid. They may be easily lulled into bad investment decisions, but they know what it feels like when they hurt, and after Americans lost half or more of their retirement in the financial meltdown, the last thing they wanted to do was put themselves even deeper in the hole by borrowing "free" money.

If Americans are ever the most skeptical, it's right after they've lost a bunch of money and seen everyone else lose it as well.

Truthfully, borrowing may not have been a bad idea. If you had borrowed $100,000 at the beginning of 2009 when the dust was beginning to settle, put it in an index fund that tracks the S&P 500 and held it to today, you'd be sitting on close to $326,000, enough to pay back the minimal interest you would have accrued from ridiculously cheap loans. Including dividends, you'd have closer to $400,000.

Of course, hindsight is 20-20. Back then, borrowing that kind of money when you were already as worried as you were about the future would have been foolish. The financial crisis was already too much of a nightmare to add any additional concern.

THIS ISN'T THE FIRST TIME

The point is, from an economic planning perspective, QE was a moronic idea from the start.

Former Chair of the Federal Reserve Ben Bernanke has praised himself for having the sense to give QE a try—to throw a bunch of darts at the wall and try to see what sticks. He says QE saved the economy. Some of us have a different opinion. Former U.S. presidential candidate and former Governor of Texas Rick Perry said of Bernanke's policies, "If this guy prints more money, I dunno what y'all would do to him in Iowa but we would treat him pretty ugly down in Texas." Printing more money to play politics at this particular time in American history is almost treasonous in my opinion."

Maybe he was just playing politics.

Maybe he was willing to try anything.

Maybe he was doing what he genuinely thought was best.

The fact of the matter is, QE failed to increase consumer confidence, which is why for the past several years this so-called "recovery" has felt more like a crawl. Perhaps it did some good. Maybe it increased consumer demand enough to improve the economy by a little bit. Or perhaps it just injected the economy with enough funny money that the next time the economy crashes, it will feel even worse. After all, what goes up, must come down.

Take Japan for example.

Japan has been experimenting with QE since their crippling recession in the late 1980s and early 1990s that saw them go from the emerging world superpower to less than a quarter and barely a third of the world's next two largest economies, the United States and China.

Ever since, Japan has been in and out of recession. Meanwhile, its nation's government has tried to revitalize its dying economy by any means necessary.

By 2014, Japan had tripled the rate of QE that its developed world peers, the United States and Europe, had attempted. And sure, it sent the stock market on a tear and actually doubled it at one point, but they took on record debt levels to do it. Japan has the highest debt-to-GDP ratio of any nation on earth. It's more than double that of the United States.

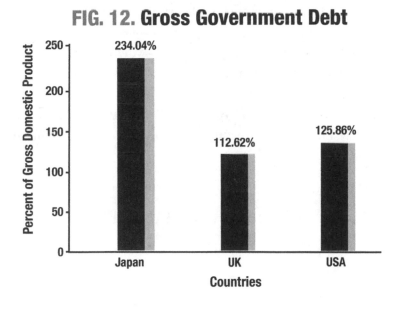

Source: Japan - OECD Data https://data.oecd.org/japan.htm

The reality is that Japan is facing massive demographic headwinds from aging and record debt levels, and QE hasn't helped.

If anything, it's made matters even worse, as Japan now has more debt and fewer people to help pay it off. In 2015, Japan (and the ECB to follow) even began experimenting with negative interest rates as another tool in the monetary playbook to help juice the economy. In a normal interest rate relationship, a bank pays you money for the pleasure of holding onto and investing your cash. Conversely, you pay the bank in interest if you take out a loan.

With negative interest rates, you pay the bank to store your money instead of the other way around. Japan and others justify it as the minimal charge you pay for a service—money is safer at the bank than it is stored in the basement, hidden under the floorboards, or buried in the backyard. At the same time, it encourages consumers to take out loans. Rather than pay the bank interest, the bank now pays *you to borrow its money*. It's crazy. It sounds great in theory. But in practice, the idea is untested, absurd, and not proven to get the economy moving.

Point is, Japan is desperate to get money flowing again. They're willing to do whatever it takes. If zero percent interest rates make money free, then negative interest rates make money somehow "more than free." And if free money was too good to be true and caused borrowers to stay away, I don't know what they think more than free will be able to achieve.

THE CORPORATE HANDOUT

Of course, QE was successful in achieving one thing.

Remember those buybacks I told you about?

QE is exactly what gave corporations the window of opportunity they needed to borrow as much money as humanly possible and use it to prop up their stocks in the open market.

Remember, CEOs and other corporate executives are always re-warded—in cold hard cash—whenever their stocks outperform the market. To them, it's more important that earnings *seem* good, not so much that they actually are good (up to a certain point).

With Main Street America crippled by the financial collapse, Wall Street saw the opportunity to gobble up all the gains for themselves, putting more money in the pockets of the people who caused the financial crisis in the first place, and sending stocks blowing past record highs in the second longest bull market in U.S. history.

Essentially, Wall Street saw an opportunity and they ran with it.

That's all well and good if you've been in the market and enjoyed the gains alongside them.

But economically speaking, it's a disaster waiting to happen.

It's one thing if stock market prices increased due to market-related reasons. A company's stock might go up because sales have improved, or because they've carved out a new section of the market and found

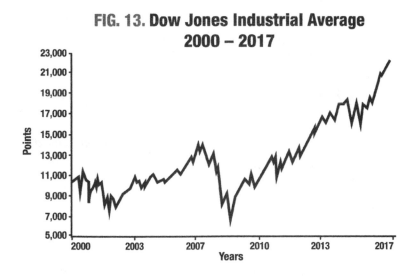

FIG. 13. Dow Jones Industrial Average 2000 – 2017

Source: Macrotrends - http://www.macrotrends.net/1319/dow-jones-100-year-historical-chart

new customers to buy their products. When that happens, the stock goes up, and investors reward them further by buying even more of their stock.

However, corporate buybacks are a completely different story. With buybacks, a company's stock price doesn't go up because it's financials improved. It went up because the company made its earnings *look* better by spreading them out across fewer shares. While it's good for a stock's price and good for investors up to a point—after all, it rewards investors and encourages them to keep their money invested in the business— share buybacks can be abused by using them to hide deterioration in a company's business. Essentially, it's a mirage. It's all smoke and mirrors.

Wall Street isn't blind to this, either.

They're collectively ignoring it to ride the gravy train higher.

There will come a time when the jig is up and companies are no longer able to resort to these financial shenanigans. The number of shares being repurchased is already starting to decrease. Again, the buybacks have been the single greatest force catapulting the market higher. If the number of buybacks drops much further, there's a chance it will carry the entire market down with it.

There's a good chance that's exactly what will happen.

A CATASTROPHE WAITING TO HAPPEN

While the number of share buybacks has never quite reached its 2007 peak during this bull run, the debt that has been used to fuel it has never been higher.

I'm talking about margin debt.

Margin debt has a history of peaking right before financial meltdowns like the ones in 2000 and in 2008.

Margin debt essentially is the debt an investor or company takes on to fund stock purchases. To do this, they essentially borrow money from their brokerage account. This is money they don't currently have, or money that is tied up in other purchases. This is what we mean when we say that QE and zero percent interest rates allowed companies to buy back their own stocks for next to nothing. It was the easiest way to increase stock values, so corporations took on as much debt as they could manage. It happened in 2000 and again in 2008.

Only this time, it's much, much worse than either of those two periods.

In 2000, margin debt levels peaked at $279 billion.

In 2008, they topped out again at $381 billion.

Today, margin debt has rocketed to more than $539 billion, a 41 percent increase from the financial gobbledygook in 2008 that caused all the economies on earth to enter a financial tailspin.

This is a catastrophe waiting to happen.

It simply isn't sustainable.

FIG. 14. United States Margin Debt

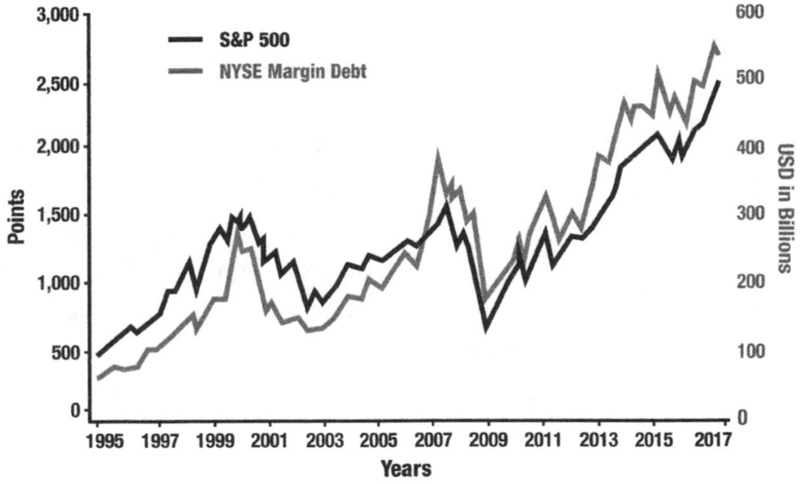

Source: topdowncharts.com

Corporations have too much debt to keep up this practice of artificially juicing their stock prices for much longer. To really drive this point home, take a look at this next chart.

This chart shows the correlation between peak margin debt levels and financial catastrophe. The conclusion is immediately clear. In the year 2000 when margin debt levels collapsed, it carried the stock market down with it. The same thing happened again in 2008. And it will happen again today.

For a while there, it looked like it could happen back in 2015. Back then, the stock market was in the middle of a near two-year period where stocks went nowhere, right before the election of Donald Trump when stocks rocketed higher. But today, margin debt stands at record levels right alongside the stock market.

How high can they go?

It's anyone's guess.

But it's definitely playing with fire.

As I mentioned before with the population issue, it's unlikely we will experience another baby boom anytime in the next several years. Even if we do we wouldn't feel the economic benefits of it for years and even decades to come.

Similarly, it's unlikely that another economic force will come to lift the tide after buybacks and margin debt give out. It's possible that American corporations could look overseas to expand their markets. Unfortunately, that also seems unlikely. Recent political shakeups like Brexit and the U.S. presidential election show a wide dissatisfaction with the globalized economy or "globalization," the trend toward businesses operating all over the globe and looking overseas for new customers but also cheaper labor. We see this through various factors, such as the recent backlash against immigration, voters who lost their jobs to overseas labor (who, dissatisfied with our politicians in Washington, looked to candidates such as Donald Trump and Bernie Sanders as their champions), and many others.

Today, multinational American corporations already earn as much as half of their revenues overseas. As the globalization trend winds down, it's likely this will affect stock valuations as well.

IT'S TIME TO GET REAL

All in all, I hope I have been able to help educate you as to some of the arguments against the bullish case for U.S. stocks. From population decline and business slowdown, to the artificial engineering of a third stock bubble via ultra-low interest rates and debt, there are numerous pieces of evidence to argue the case that now is *not* the time to invest in U.S. equities.

I know some may find that hard to swallow. Stocks have blown past every estimate over the past year, marching higher and higher to a seemingly infinite destination. Will the Dow climb to 25,000? All the way to 30,000? Even 50,000?

Quit dreaming.

If you are age 55 or above, and either preparing for retirement, about ready to enter, or already settled in, there is no reasonable evidence to believe equities can continue to keep up the pace we've seen since November 2016.

I understand Americans love to gamble. Who doesn't on some level? The idea of getting something for absolutely nothing (with the help of a little luck) is enough to get anyone to throw away their cash.

But consider this. The stock market has climbed 20 percent since November 2016. It could have perhaps another 10, 15, or 20 percent left in it.

Now consider this. Let's say the market suffers a 5 percent drop in the coming weeks. From there, let's say it drops another 10 percent, and from there, keeps dropping. Before you know it, the market has fallen all the way back to its 2007 highs—a 36 percent drop from right now.

That's a reasonable, and conservative estimation.

When bubbles deflate, they usually return to the peak gains of the last bubble. That, or they fall all the way back to the start of the most recent bubble or lower.

Let's say the latter happened and the market fell all the way to its 2009 lows. In March 2009, the S&P 500 bottomed at 683. Considering these drops tend to get sequentially larger one after the other, it would probably drop a little farther. It's not guaranteed, but it's very much in the realm of possibility. After all, the market dropped more during the financial crisis than it did during the tech bust. In a situation where the market fell all the way beneath its 2009 lows, we would be looking at a 75 percent loss of today's market values.

The Great Recession saw stock investors lose 58 percent of their money and that was already bad enough. Imagine another meltdown where the onslaught is even worse. Consumption would dry up as demand for goods and services ceases. Companies would go out of business. Civil unrest might even erupt as people demand harsh regulations against the Wall Street machine that destroyed their financial lives three times already in this century.

Could you handle it?

Could your financial portfolio handle it?

Would it threaten your ability to retire?

These are serious questions I want you to ask that are critical to your financial well-being.

I understand some may wish to believe the market may continue to climb higher. Maybe they're right. Maybe the market goes up another 20 percent from today's levels.

But think about it like this. If this were a poker game, and you had to bet $75 for the chance of earning $20, would you make the bet?

Of course not.

Maybe you would make that bet when you were younger and had time to lose.

If you are anywhere close to retirement, there simply is no time left. We're entering the fourth quarter. Now's the time to hunker down and get serious about retirement.

That is the perspective you need to have as a retiree or pre-retiree today.

Now is the time to stay vigilant.

Rather than try to squeeze out every last drop of this bull run before it dries up, it's time to switch your financial game plan to a more prudent, defensive strategy—one that focuses on income, not growth.

You don't want to play Wall Street's game anymore. This is a dance with the devil you can't win. Large, institutional investors like them will always have a seat at the table no matter how bad the markets get. Ordinary, Main Street investors don't have the same advantage. If you suffer a 75 percent loss of your money, it's game over. It's called "the house always wins."

Trust me, you don't want to be caught with the bag when the party comes to a screeching halt.

Ask yourself: how lucky do you feel?

Lucky enough to bet the house?

Lucky enough to go for broke?

Go right ahead. I wish you the best of luck.

But I promise you—if you focus your financial strategy toward holding onto the gains you've already made, and going for smaller, more conservative gains (as opposed to larger, more aggressive ones) to offset your withdrawals in retirement, you will end up *much* richer than if you keep your money in the market at today's levels. Remember, even a one-year, 20 percent drawdown can radically alter your retirement and cost you hundreds of thousands of dollars over the lifetime of your portfolio.

A FINAL LOOK

Let's take one last look at why now is not the time to put any significant portion of your retirement in the market at today's levels.

Earlier we confronted the notion that the stock market always goes up over the long term. It's correct, so long as you define the "long term" as a really, really long term. Over a shorter timeframe, investors can lose over half their portfolio—like the two years in between 2007 and 2009 when the stock market lost more than half its value, the 13 years between 2000 and 2013 when the market failed to achieve a new high, or the 25 years it took for stocks to recover from their 1929 crash. We also discussed how financial advisers are willing to tell you anything you want to hear to get you into the market and put more money into their pockets and the pockets of the firms they work for.

But let's take a much wider look—a 30,000-foot view of the history of the stock market to get a more precise look at what we can expect in the next five years or so.

THE STOCK MARKET AT 30,000 FEET

The Dow Jones Industrial Average dates all the way back to 1896 when the index was first created. It consists of 30 significant stocks that are representative of the broader American economy. There are no specific rules for which stocks are included, and the 30 stocks are selected by the editors of *The Wall Street Journal* newspaper. While the index dates back to the end of the nineteenth century, we have data for the U.S. stock market that goes back more than 200 years.

Yes, I'm going way back.

Wall Street *is* very *present*-focused. They only want stocks to go up and assume they always do. They're bad at using the past to

FIG. 15. Stock Market 1901-Present

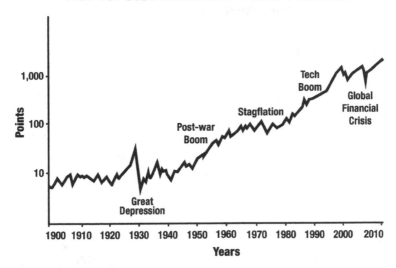

Source: Macrotrends - http://www.macrotrends.net/1319/dow-jones-100-year-historical-chart

make an educated guess of the future. They never learn from their mistakes.

Typically, I only take the 35-year view. That's about how long it takes for stocks to go through their secular market cycle, meaning how long it takes stocks to cycle through one bear market and one bull market.

But when you take a maximum view of the stock market, and look over the more than 200 years of stock market history, common sense starts to kick in, and you begin to realize how puny and insignificant this whole debate is. You see how insignificant each year and even each 5- to 10-year period is to the overall history of the market, which enables you to take a very objective and undiluted view of the present.

Not only that, you start to witness some very obvious patterns that are clear as day.

The entire history of the stock market is a series of cycles. Stocks move up, down, and sideways in successive, lyrical rhythm.

The progressive era was a 30-year period in U.S. history that saw stocks run virtually flat, with intermittent up and down moves in between.

Next came the Roaring Twenties, a time of great prosperity and advancement that saw the emergence of new technologies such as the automobile, the radio, and aviation. Stocks handed investors several hundred and thousand percent winners.

Next came another 25-year period of stocks going nowhere, crashing, and eventually recovering over a period that spanned the Great Depression, World War II, and the birth of the baby boomer generation.

A post-war boom followed, taking the market to new highs for the first time in a generation. Enter the 1970s and stocks entered a period of stagflation where stocks moved sideways. Then came the great boom of the 1980s and 1990s that saw the market rise over 1,000 percent, the greatest and longest boom in our nation's history.

That brings us to this millennium. Save a few years of market euphoria here and there, the 21st century has been a time of economic uncertainty for investors, featuring two devastating crashes, each of which rival the market crash that preceded the Great Depression itself.

Do you see the patterns of waves and cycles?

Do you see how insignificant another few months or years of gains are?

Every 35 to 40 years or so, the market goes through a volatile, intense period of up and down movements that, overtime, has ultimately carried it higher. Each of those longer cycles contain two distinct bull and bear markets that terrify and amaze investors, subjecting us to a roller coaster ride of fear and hope that, in the grand scheme of things, leaves us better off. Clearly, over the long term, stocks really do go up!

Young investors would do well to heed this. While I wouldn't necessarily recommend putting all their money into the market at today's levels, it's important to understand that strong buying opportunities will present themselves in the years ahead. (If you haven't tutored your sons, daughters, nieces, and nephews on this fact, I highly encourage you to do so while they're still young. Show them this chart. Show them everything you achieved and how it enabled you to provide for you and them. It's one of the best lessons you can teach your children to motivate them to be able to someday provide for themselves.)

But it's important to maintain perspective. If you invested through the 1980s and 1990s, and survived the crashes of 2000 and 2008 and remained invested through today, you've done incredibly well for yourself. But that can only be the case if you do not lose what you have, right now, while the market is still at or near its all-time highs.

It's as simple as that.

No ifs, ands, or buts.

If you weren't in the markets at all the right times, that's okay. No one can time the market perfectly. As a warm-blooded American who was alive to witness the greatest growth period in this great nation's history, I know that may be difficult to stomach. We feel personally obligated to soak up every last cent the market is willing to give us. We feel, despite the better angels of our nature, that it is our God-given right. And we all understand, on some level that the stock market is the single greatest vehicle for social advancement in this country. It can create a legacy that lasts for generations from a single stock if you time things perfectly. For example, had you bought Cisco Systems early on in 1990 and held to its peak in 2000, you would have seen a 200,000 percent increase on your money, enough to turn a small, $5,000 investment into $10 million.

But it's stories like these that can be both tempting but also deceiving. Greed can cause even the wisest men to think irrationally at times. The truth is there's less than a one in a million chance you'll ever bank that much from a single stock or even a portfolio of stocks. On average, the stock market returns 8 to 10 percent per year over the very, very long term, say 35 years or more. Individual stock pickers—

those who think they can outperform the market by picking the best of the best stocks—tend to earn much less because outguessing the market is actually very difficult. Only folks like Warren Buffett have been able to do it over an extended period of time, and even he loses some years.

The truth is that the majority of stocks fail over the long term. In fact, if you look at the entire universe of stocks in the 25-year period between 1983 and 2007, you'll find some interesting statistics:

- Over that time, the Russell 3000, or the index that measures the top 3,000 stocks or the majority of stocks in the market, delivered investors a 500 percent return on their money.[6]
- However, of those stocks, 64 percent of those stocks underperformed,
- 39 percent of them outright declined,
- And 19 percent declined by at least 75 percent or more, wiping out most of their gains.
- Meanwhile, *just 25 percent of the stocks in the Russell 3000 accounted for all of the markets gains.*
- The remaining 11 percent were virtually flat.

In other words, over a 25-year period, you had a one in four chance in making *any* gains on a single stock.

After a certain point, don't you just want to be done with it all? Aren't you sick of spinning the roulette wheel? Tired of the corporate greed and being a part of Wall Street's system?

IT'S TIME TO GET OUT OF THE MARKET

As I've made clear before, the goal of Wall Street and the financial advisers who work for them is not to advise you, it's to sell to you. They do not have your best interests at heart. They don't advocate for you in a way that will preserve and grow your retirement for the long haul or protect you from the financial devastation that another crash will bring. And they are certainly aren't equipped to educate you about the history of the stock market and what a long-term view of the market could mean for the next 5 to 10 years.

The truth is that the only stock still in the Dow Jones Industrial Average—the universe of the top 30 stocks in the market—from its start over 100 years ago is General Electric, and even it has cycled in and out of the index over that time. Since then, dozens and even hundreds of stocks have stood alongside it, cycling in and out of the index. To think, a portfolio of even the best, most robust companies in the market can still be subject to such volatility!

Who wants to play a game with those kind of odds?

No one preparing for retirement should.

The reality is that the entire system is stacked against you. The entire Wall Street operation is a sham. It's time to move on—time to put your hard-earned money into a portfolio of defensive assets that throw a reasonable interest or dividend every year to reward you for your prudence and help you sleep better and easier in retirement.

Hopefully I've convinced you. Investing according to the way I advocate requires a critical change in perspective. Most investors haven't been trained or taught to think in this way. They've seen staggering bull markets, and crushing bear markets, and been told by an army of Wall Street analysts that the market always wins. But it's important to keep perspective. If you've amassed enough wealth to carry yourself through to retirement, it's time to quit the "old way" of investing.

Of course, you won't quit—you'll just retire and do something else. You'll switch your investment strategy to a fundamentally different approach that will continue to grow your nest egg, conservatively, over the next 5, 10, 20 years or more—whatever your timeline—while preserving the legacy you've built for yourself.

Now is the time to practice common sense. It's time to wake up from the financial dream Wall Street has tried to sell you all your life. If you're age 55 or above, retirement is coming faster than you can possibly realize. It may already be here for you. If that's the case, now's not the time to risk everything in the market. It's not the time to risk your and your family's future. Either way, I can practically assure you that switching to an income-oriented financial strategy through the rest of your days will actually see your assets grow *larger* than if you just bought and held the market the way Wall Street wants you to.

I believe it's a win-win. I've protected and raised tens of millions of dollars for my clients by investing with discipline, not gut instinct. I can do the same for you as well. In the next few chapters, I'll show you how.

4

The Importance of Yield in the Age of QE

RETIREMENT IS A relatively new phenomenon. It's only been around for the past one hundred years or so. It's not too surprising then that we're still working out some of the kinks. Today, we think of retirement as a thing everyone gets to do someday. The reality is much different. It sounds reasonable that if we spend our whole lives working to become productive members of society, we should get a break in our old age. But just because something makes sense doesn't mean it's actually so. The truth is that retirement, for many, is a luxury they'll never be able to attain.

A look at some retirement statistics puts a few things into perspective:

- 45 percent of Americans have nothing saved for retirement.
- The average American age 50-year-old American has just $42,797 in retirement savings. In order to retire "successfully" by industry standards, he or she will need to amass roughly $1 million—or $957,203 over the next 15 years. That's how much you will need to maintain your lifestyle and enjoy a comfortable retirement for 20 years or more.
- 36 percent of American adults over the age of 65 are completely dependent on Social Security, and 63 percent are de-

pendent on a combination of Social Security, friends, relatives, and charity.

- The Social Security Administration is slowly running out of money, and reports that by 2034 it will only be able to pay 77 percent of its promised distributions.

- The maximum monthly Social Security payment for a person retiring today is $2,687 per month, a healthy sum. But the average is just $1,342, which comes out to roughly $16,104 a year in benefits. Again, as many as one third of retirees are entirely dependent on this meager amount.

- The average out-of-pocket medical costs—meaning those not covered by Medicare or your health insurance—will be $218,000 over the next 20 years.[7]

You don't need a degree in mathematics to realize these numbers don't line up.

If a person only has $40,000 in retirement at the age of 50, there's no way they'll reach $1 million by the time they hit 65. They'll be lucky to hit $250,000.

If the average retiree collects $16,000 a year in benefits, over 20 years they can expect to collect roughly $320,000. But if $218,000 will be eaten by medical costs, that leaves just over $100,000. Divide that over 20 years and it's just $5,000 a year to cover expenses that aren't medical. That might cover the groceries. But what about utilities? TV and Internet? Your phone? What if you have a mortgage payment? What if your car needs maintenance?

It's clear that we have a retirement crisis in America without a good solution.

That's because the whole idea of retirement has never been fully thought out.

THE BIRTH OF RETIREMENT

We don't spend a lot of time thinking about this, but humans haven't exactly "evolved" to retire. Until the past couple hundred years or so, retirement didn't even exist. You worked until you died or until you couldn't work anymore. That was it.

Of course, support systems were in place. It used to be common for families of multiple generations to live together and provide social and economic support for one another. When one generation grew too old to work, they passed those duties on to the younger generation. Economies of the past didn't allow for the upward mobility we have today, so a child born on a farm would probably spend his or her whole life working and dying on that farm. At the very least, the family would be able to support each other.

It wasn't until fairly recently that, as technologies like the steam engine and the automobile have made travel and transportation easier, these multi-generational families split up, with the younger members looking for opportunities hundreds or even thousands of miles away when they came of age. When the younger generation leaves to pursue opportunities elsewhere, it leaves no one to care for the elderly in their old age. Someone else—namely government—has to step in.

Enter the age of retirement.

With an elderly class now left to more or less fend for itself, governments began experimenting with the idea of a "social safety net" for its most dependent citizens—those who were too old or too weak to work and provide for themselves.

The first retirement pensions were introduced in 1889 by the Prussian statesman Otto von Bismarck. As time went on, the idea of providing financial security for the elderly spread across the globe, expanding across Europe, the U.S., and other countries.

WHY NOW?

Why did it take so long for a concept like retirement to take place?

The answer: human population and the birth of democracy. I realize that's a mouthful. I'll explain.

Essentially, as human population has expanded, governments have found themselves with more and more people to provide for. As more democratic systems of government took place, the people—who hold the power in a democratic system—demanded help in their old age.

In the past, when economies were weaker and less industrialized, governments and monarchies would simply enslave the lower classes or place them into "indentured servitude" (a fancy word for slavery).

But with the birth of democracy, governments suddenly became beholden to the people, and so did the politicians who worked for them (that is, at least, when government is done right). If the people were unhappy, they could revolt and vote them all out.

It's difficult to talk about politics today and I don't really want to get into that. This is a book about how to advance your retirement strategy. But it's important to understand how we got to where we are today when it comes to standards of living and retirement.

The standard of living wasn't as high as it is today. That, and retirement is a relatively new concept and only works if economies are healthy. It's only by making democracy and capitalism work together that our economy can work as it's meant to. And it's only when our economy works as it's meant to that a system like retirement can actually take place.

This is key. Capitalism makes people richer. Democracy, meanwhile, works to make sure everyone has a seat at the table. Overtime, this necessitated a system like retirement. If people were going to work harder to create a better society for everyone, they expected to be compensated in their old age. And if capitalism ever goes too far too fast and greed takes over, democracy is there to help right the ship.

That's exactly what happened during the Great Depression.

By the end of the Roaring Twenties, stocks had become so over-bought that when the selling commenced and the market keeled over, it dragged America's economy down with it, leading to the worst depression in our nation's history.

To make up for it, the U.S. government created the Social Security Administration to offer Americans a safety net.

When the first Social Security checks were mailed out in January 1940, lifespans were nowhere near what they are today. Americans were lucky to see the age of 65. If they reached it, the U.S. government stepped in to offer financial assistance to help them wind down their affairs for just a handful of years. (Ironically, the first Social Security beneficiary, Ida May Fuller, didn't live for just a handful of years after she turned 65. She lived to be 100 years old. The funny part is she didn't start paying into Social Security until she was 62 when the system went into place. She paid a total of $24 for three years before she began to receive benefits. Her first check was for $22—almost as much as she had paid in three years. By time she died, she had collected close to $21,000, or 864 times more than she paid in. If only we all were so lucky!)

A SECOND RETIREMENT BENEFIT?

Fast forward a few years. Following World War II, companies began to offer their own entitlement benefits. After years of sluggish economic growth through the 1930s and the Great Depression, America's economy was ready to take off.

The problem was, there wasn't nearly enough labor. After years of hiring freezes, suddenly, companies couldn't seem to hire *enough* workers. To attract more labor, they began introducing a new form of entitlement: pensions.

Pensions are a dirty word today because they're going out of style. Back then, they were all the rage. Rather than just earn a wage, workers would receive an additional payment that would be paid by the company years later when they chose to retire. Now they would receive both Social Security *and* a pension.

Years later pensions would become the massive problem they are today. Remember—something that seems too good to be true usually is. But, so long as companies were offering them, workers naturally took the bait.

Over the next several decades, pensions became the new trend. If you wanted to attract the most competitive workers, you not only had to offer a competitive wage, you had to include a pension on top of it.

It worked—right up until it didn't.

In 1940, approximately 12 percent of workers had pensions. By 1955, the number shot up to 32 percent.[8] Then by the 1970s, when 55 percent of American workers had a pension, companies realized they had overextended themselves and were desperate to get rid of the things. They suddenly realized they couldn't keep their promises—it was too expensive to pay for everyone.

At some level, this is just capitalism.

Companies are all about making money. If they have excess money available, it makes more sense to invest it in their growing business so the company can continue to grow into the future. One way to invest in their business is to hire the best workers and do whatever they can to attract them. That, or they can turn the money over to their shareholders in the form of a dividend payment to keep their stocks prices up. In an ideal world, they'd offer and be able to pay pensions for all their workers on top of that. But the world is not an ideal place. Business has gotten more competitive. Companies are fighting to stay ahead, pushing and shoving to be the best in their industries. Putting money aside for pension benefits just makes those companies less competitive and less able to put their money toward productive measures. (Of course, corporate buybacks show that isn't always their priority. Business management teams are more concerned with padding their own pockets than they are the workers who keep the company going. Hence, why we've seen CEO salaries go up 1,000 percent over the last 40 years while the middle class has stagnated).

THE PENSION PROBLEM

Essentially, offering pension benefits was easy so long as the economy was booming. Money kept flowing into companies and companies could thereby afford to turn some of that money over to their workers.

But whenever the economy entered a down period, it wasn't so simple. In a bear market, companies have to fight just to survive. Adding a pension on top of that? That becomes a millstone around their head.

That brings us to where we are today.

Today, pension funds are running out of money. Millions of company pensions are under threat because employees are retiring earlier and living longer. The longer they live, the more the company has to pay. And improved lifestyles means that pension promises that were made in the 1970s and 1980s have become too expensive to keep.

Take the state of Illinois, home of Chicago, for instance. The state's pension is only 43.4 percent funded. That means they only have enough money to cover less than half of their obligations.[9] And that's just the worst example. As of 2014, only two states have fully funded pension programs: South Dakota and Wisconsin.

Meanwhile, Social Security barely covers the bills with an average annual payout worth just $16,000. That's why retirees and governments are looking for a solution. Market research shows that four out of 10 recent retirees relied on more than half of their retirement through

FIG. 16. 10 Most Underfunded State Pensions

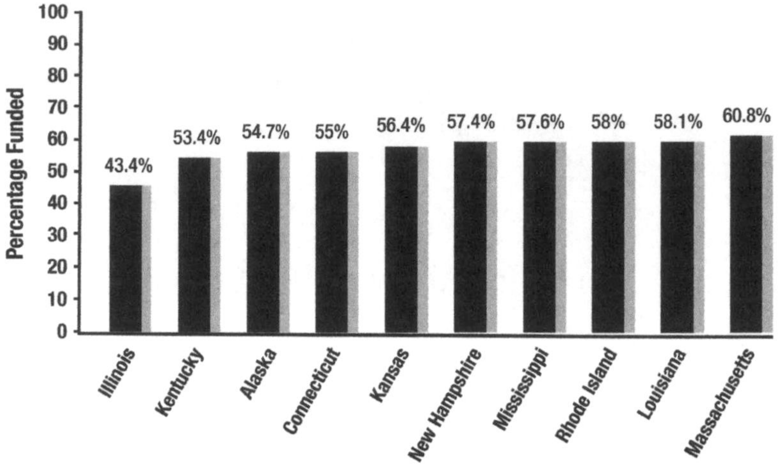

Source: partial ALM Media, LLC. The Street & https://www.bloomberg.com/search?query=
10+states+with+the+most+underfunded+pensions&endTime=2017-09-24T00:34:58.945Z&page=1

their pension. Only one in four baby boomers expect the same in retirement, meaning 75 percent of the current retiring population will need to find another form of guaranteed income to fill the void. As time goes on and pensions completely run out of money, that figure will rise to 100 percent.

401(k)s and IRAs emerged to turn the burden of retirement back over to the people. But as a society, we don't educate our people on how best to prepare for this eventuality. We basically leave people to fend for themselves. Not only that, but corporate America is always looking to find new ways to get you to part with your hard-earned cash.

We need a better way.

TAKING BACK RETIREMENT

For decades, retirement has been a very black and white concept. You work most of your life. You save and save and save. You reach 65, and then you stop. If you've done everything as you should, you'll have enough money set aside to live off of until you die.

It sounds simple, but it's not.

Americans are great at spending. We spend most of our income on things like rent, mortgages, groceries, motor vehicles, movies, vacations, etc.

But we're terrible at saving.

The American family averages about $5,000 in retirement savings.[10] Retirement, for most Americans, is light years away, a dream that will never become reality because there's no one holding a gun to our head every month telling us to put some money away each month for when we retire.

Yet, the entire financial planning industry is built around this very concept—that Americans are great at practicing financial self-discipline, when in fact they're anything but. Take for example our bloated government, which is now $20 trillion in debt. As a culture, we've created this idea that we can pay with money we don't actually have. It's no wonder then that we have a retirement crisis in America. We think money grows on trees.

I'm all for self-sufficiency and reliance. I think entitlements are necessary but also problematic since entitlements teach people to be lazy. It's best to approach retirement from the perspective that you are entitled to nothing.

But the harsh truth is, saving up enough money for retirement is *hard*.

First of all, how much is enough?

$500,000?

$750,000?

$1 million?

$2 million? (After all, a million dollars isn't what it used to be.)

We have this idea that we're supposed to spend our entire lives building up this "nest egg" that eventually hatches and allows us to live out our golden years.

But what does that actually look like?

How much should you set aside each year?

$10,000?

$15,000?

$34,000?

There's no one right answer, and that's what makes it difficult. Everyone has different lifestyles and different needs when it comes to retirement. What works for one person might not work for another.

Then there's the question of whether most Americans are even comfortable with the idea of putting money into an account they can't touch for 20, 30, or even 40 years. Most people are too paranoid for that. With a government that has $20 trillion in debt and markets that seem to crash every few years or so, who can blame them? Putting money somewhere you can't touch and hoping to see it again in 40 years seems like a gamble.

THE 4 PERCENT RULE

The goal for retirement, of course, is to never run out of money. That's what makes the nest egg approach hard. You think you have enough, but you never really know until you actually start to spend it all.

For years, financial planners have used the idea of the "4 percent rule" to guide retirees about how to spread their nest egg through retirement. Essentially, the 4 percent rule states that you should withdraw

4 percent of your portfolio each year for living expenses. If you have a portfolio worth $1 million, 4 percent would be $40,000. That's how much you could withdraw each year.

But there's a problem.

If you start at age 65 and withdraw $40,000 every year, that adds up quickly.

By the end of year one, your $1 million is now $960,000.

By year five, it's $750,000.

By year 10, you're down to $500,000—half the value of your original portfolio.

At this rate, by the time you hit 85, you will have spent every last cent of your $1 million.

If you only live to age 82, great! You dodged the bullet.

But what if you live to be 86? Would you want to live your last year on earth poor and destitute?

What if you live longer?

What if you live to be 88? 90? 100?

NO HARD AND FAST RULES, JUST GUIDELINES

This is why the 4 percent rule doesn't work. Unless you plan on dying at a certain age (a position no one should have to be put in), you have to make some adjustments.

Financial planners have recently amended the 4 percent rule to a new 2 percent rule. Presumably, it doubles the amount of time you have until your money runs out. But it also means you have less to work with each year.

But it's not just the financial constraints that are a problem. There's a psychological factor as well.

When you're 65 and you have $1 million sitting in the bank and you've just retired, you're probably feeling pretty good.

By age 70, you're down by a quarter. There's this nagging thought in the back of your head that you could run out of money, but you can choose to ignore it.

By age 75, that nagging thought is no longer so easy to ignore.

You've only been retired 10 years and you've already spent half your money. You're starting to freak out, and rightfully so. By the time you turn 85, you'll have nothing left to live on.

No one should have to live *hoping* they die by a certain age.

The goal shouldn't be to plan your death. Your goal should be to live a good, long, healthy life and set an example for your children (and the whole human race for that matter) to live as long as you possibly can. You can't do that if you're worrying about money the whole time. The whole point of retirement is that you shouldn't have to worry about money in the first place. It's supposed to be your big break! Not your big burden.

THE NEW RETIREMENT

This is why the financial planning industry is moving away from the nest egg approach to what we call a more "holistic" approach.

The goal shouldn't be to make a huge sum of money and slowly chip away at it until you die.

The goal is to make enough money by the time you retire to be able to *pay yourself* to be able to maintain the lifestyle you have today. Paying yourself doesn't take wealth. It takes income.

With an income approach, your lifestyle doesn't have to change. That's important to people. Our lifestyles are a reflection of who we are as people. If you're working, your income allows you to enjoy the lifestyle you have right now. If you wish to maintain that lifestyle worry-free, you have to keep the money flowing once you retire. You have to figure out a way to keep money coming into the bank without having to sit at a desk for 40 hours a week.

The goal for retirement then doesn't become about making a huge sum of money. It's about making enough money to be able to *make your retirement work for you.*

It's not so much a change in strategy as it is a change in mindset.

In the previous example, a 65-year-old retiree with $1 million plans to withdraw $40,000 a year for living expenses. Obviously, he would choose to invest the remaining $960,000 to try to offset the $40,000 he was losing.

But by changing your mindset from one that requires one big obscure number to one that requires a set amount of income to maintain your present lifestyle, it makes everything easier.

Now you don't have to worry about spending down your entire net worth.

Now your net worth doesn't even play a factor in your retirement.

By continuing to invest your retirement in such a way that you can live off the *income* from your investments, you'll never have to worry about running out of money. Ideally, you'll never lose your money in the first place. By the time you die, you'd still have that $1 million to be able to pass down to your children.

Maybe you don't want to leave your children that much. Maybe you'd be comfortable leaving them half or a quarter of that through an inheritance fund. Perhaps you'd give another portion of it to a nonprofit or to a charity. Or maybe you'd spend some more of your principal simply enjoying your retirement—sailing around the world, visiting exotic locations, and rediscovering yourself in your old age.

By all means. At the end of the day, it's your money. But if you're going to spend your money, it should be on things you want to spend it on. It shouldn't go toward basic costs such as groceries and medical payments. That's what income is for. A more holistic, income-oriented retirement strategy therefore allows you to live off the money your investments generate, so you don't actually have to spend a thing just to survive.

If you like the way that sounds, you're not alone.

This is the direction the entire retirement and financial planning industries are eventually headed. As more and more baby boomers say "Enough!" with the stock market and switch to investments that pay them an income, Wall Street will have to contend with this. Their days of preaching that growth and risk are the end all and be all are over. Americans wants a sound, secure retirement. Not a risky, uncertain one.

HOW WE GOT HERE

This is, of course, all easier said than done. Nothing in this life is free. You have to work for it, but the benefits are rewarding.

For starters, the market is changing. Investors aren't switching to income-oriented strategies for no reason. Two 50 percent crashes and decades of financial turmoil have ruined a lot of people's appetites for risk. People want to protect what they have rather than risk losing it at the casino.

But the market is also once again at record highs. There simply isn't that much "value" left in the market. Most competing industries have peaked. Some sectors are still advancing, such as tech stocks and more speculative investments like marijuana and bitcoin, but many of these investments are too volatile for a person aged 65 or older. Someone that age doesn't want to wake up the next day to see a 5, 10, or 20 percent decrease on their investment in a single day.

All in all, the market is just too expensive. Conservative, income-oriented investors have to look elsewhere beyond traditional stocks to meet their needs.

Dividend stocks aren't necessarily the best bet either. For decades retirees have relied on older, bigger, proven companies that have survived through years of booms and busts that pay their loyal investors a solid dividend in retirement.

The problem is, dividend stocks all went down the last time the market crashed. Sure, they might throw off a 4 or 5 percent dividend each year if you're lucky. But many dividend stocks crashed 40, 50, even 60 percent or more in the last crash, which is exactly the kind of scenario you're trying to avoid in retirement. Financial planners for years have assured their clients that dividend stocks are a safe bet. They might be safer than the alternative growth stocks. But the difference between being dead-dead and a little dead is just semantics. At the end of the day, you're still dead.

INCOME IN THE AGE OF QUANTITATIVE EASING

This is where an income-oriented retirement plan gets tricky. If growth stocks are out, and dividend stocks are no good, what's an income investor to do? The problem grows even more complicated when you consider the present interest rate environment, because that means most bonds are out, too.

In response to the financial crisis, the Federal Reserve slashed interest rates to zero to try to jumpstart the economy. They hoped lower borrowing rates would drive more people and businesses to spend.

When that didn't work, they launched one wave of QE after the next to drive interest rates down even further, hoping that if people saw that the government would support new borrowing and lending that they would be more willing to spend.

Eight years into the recovery and interest rates are still next to zero. With each passing year, the Federal Reserve sets expectations that they will increase rates back to "normal," only to fall short on their

FIG. 17. US 10-Year Government Bond Yield

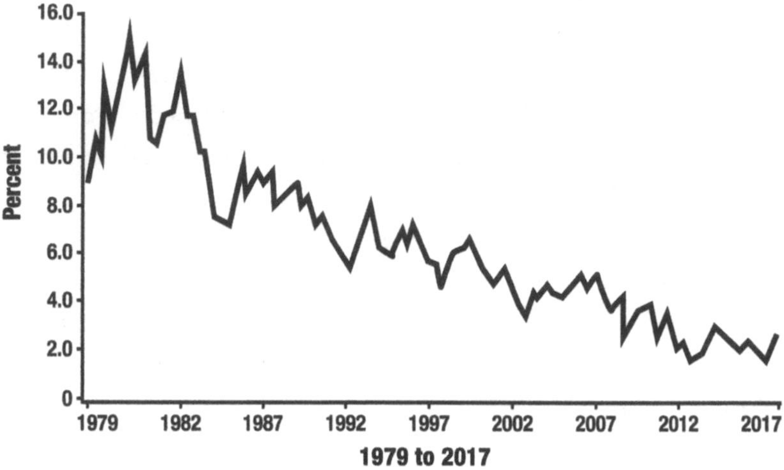

Source: OECD, "Main Economic Indicators – complete database," Main Economic
Indicators (database), http://dx.doi.org/10.1787/data-00052-en
Copyright, 2016, OECD. Reprinted with permission.

promises, talking themselves in circles while the economy continues to piddle along.

It's all politics. The fact of the matter is, low rates are here to stay. Perhaps they'll return to something resembling "normal" someday, but that day is way off. For retirees, it's time to settle in to the low interest rate environment and get used to it as the new normal. Until our economy vastly improves and until our government kicks it's ridiculous spending habit, the Federal Reserve can't afford to raise interest rates that much higher. For every quarter-percent rate increase, it costs the government an additional $50 billion in interest on our debt payments. The government is already $20 trillion in debt and can't agree on a budget in the first place. With higher rates, we would be effectively paying off debt with more debt. We're already doing just that, but it would only be worse.

That puts income investors in a pickle.

When the Federal Reserve slashed the overnight rate that banks pay to lend each other money, otherwise known as the fed funds rate, they lowered the yield on most income-producing investments with it. That's because the Federal Reserve effectively serves as the benchmark interest rate for everything else.

Today, savings accounts, money market funds, and certificates of deposits pay an interest rate of next to nothing.

Treasury bonds pay only a fraction of what they used to. Before the financial crisis, a 10-Year Treasury note paid between 5 and 6 percent. Now it yields just over 2 percent.

To find a decent yield, the average investor is forced into the stock market, buying stocks at all-time highs just to earn a respectable yield on their money. That leaves them vulnerable to downside risks or just general market volatility.

Fact is, investors are having a hard time finding a fixed income in today's low interest rate environment. It's gotten so difficult that as recently as June 2016 there was more than $11.7 trillion in negative interest rate bonds worldwide. That means that people invested $11.7

FIG. 18. Stock of Government Bonds Negative Yields – US Dollars

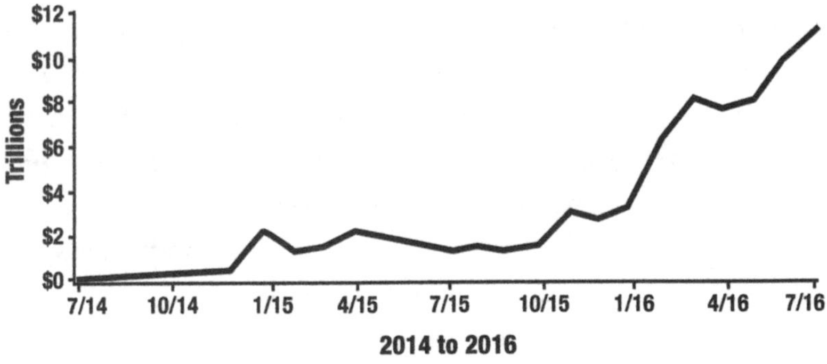

Source: Data from International Settlements

trillion in bonds that not only didn't pay them, but that they had to pay for.

So, while financial securities are hitting record highs, solid yields are getting harder and harder to find. Today's present market doesn't reward the average income investor, it rewards the growth investor. Since Donald Trump's election, the Dow Jones Industrial Average has climbed more than 20 percent. On average, stocks average 8 percent every year. The market has shifted from caution to greed. That's a mistake. This typically happens at the top of a market cycle. Investors plow in at the last minute only to be left holding the bag when the legs fall out from under them.

I'd advise you to practice caution and stick to the road less traveled. It may not be as exciting as the stock market, but investing for retirement isn't supposed to be exciting. It's supposed to be boring and without surprises. Leave the excitement to people with money to lose.

Finally, there's the issue of inflation.

A retiree might determine he needs $1 million by the age of 65 in order to retire in such a way that he can maintain his present lifestyle.

He needs 6 percent every year to account for expenses. That's $60,000 each year. Add in Social Security and any pension money and he'll have a pretty decent retirement.

But here's the problem. He'll need that $60,000 each year for the rest of his life. But $60,000 won't be worth $60,000 tomorrow. At the present rate of inflation, $60,000 will be worth closer to $50,000 by the time our retiree turns 85. If he doesn't want to eat into his principal, he'll have to earn a slightly higher rate than 6 percent each year in order to account for inflation. That's why you need to simultaneously be growing your account by reinvesting some of the interest while spending the minimum amount on your expenses.

That's what makes retirement tricky. There are no hard and fast rules. Your plans for one year of retirement may be slightly different in the next.

That's why it's important you establish a relationship with a trusted financial adviser—someone who takes a holistic approach to retirement and is willing to take time to get to know your needs and your values. There are so many individual factors to consider that, while they might be worth your time, it would be much nicer to have a professional take care of. You should be busy enjoying your retirement, not plotting it out each second while you should be living it.

That's the goal for all the clients we serve at Arbor Financial. For pre-retirees we'll work to grow your account conservatively until you retire. Once you retire, we need to take a close look at what you want to do with your money. Do you want to keep all of it invested and live solely on the income? Do you want to set up an emergency fund? Do you want to draw down on your principal a little bit every year to boost your lifestyle? We'll go through every detail to find the retirement strategy that gives you the income you need to fund your best retirement.

5

The Goldilocks Zone

FIVE PERCENT IS THE MAGIC NUMBER

WHEN I FINALLY decided to divorce myself from the big financial firms, feeling that I could never serve my clients' best interests while I stayed there, I suddenly found myself with the freedom to do things the way *I* wanted. As is the case with the typical financial adviser who's married to one of these firms, I didn't have the freedom to exercise complete control over my clients' portfolios. I was essentially only allowed to sell them on stocks and the mutual funds. Anytime money flows out of Wall Street, these big firms suffer. They don't want to accept the bull market is over until *they* say it is. Then, after they've gotten as much of Main Street's money as they can, they bolt. That's why they're not interested in selling you anything but the riskiest, most aggressive investments.

After a while, I'd had enough.

I decided to go independent primarily for two reasons:

1. I could better protect my clients running my own firm.
2. Not only could I better protect them, I could actually better help them *grow* their portfolio using strategies that are better aligned with their goals than Wall Street could.

You see, investments basically fall into three different categories.

I mentioned in the last chapter that there are two different kinds of investors—growth investors and income investors. But even these two different types fall on a spectrum.

Growth investors tend to be very aggressive. They carry the most risk. Income investors take on the least amount of risk, but in today's ultra-low interest rate environment, investing for income using traditional methods is rather tricky.

At Arbor Financial, we fall somewhere in the middle, with a bent toward the more conservative side: we want to get the most income for the least amount of risk.

Too little income isn't enough.

Too much risk is unacceptable.

We're looking for the "Goldilocks Zone." For those unfamiliar with the term, it's an idea that derives its name for the children's story "Goldilocks and the Three Bears." While Goldilocks is wandering through the woods, she stumbles upon a house with no one home. She finds three bowls of soup. Hungry, she eats a spoonful of the first bowl. Too hot. She eats a spoonful of the second. Too cold. But the third one is the right temperature.

That's exactly what we're looking for. The right amount of income for the right amount of risk. No more, no less. As Goldilocks's says in the story: "Just right."

The different kinds of investments can be lumped into three different categories: conservative, moderate, and aggressive.

The chart on the next page breaks it down.

TYPES OF INVESTMENT RISK

At the far end of the spectrum are the aggressive investments. These are the products Wall Street wants you to buy. This is what plays into their

FIG. 19.

CONSERVATIVE	MODERATE	AGGRESSIVE
Certificate of Deposit	Preferred Stock	Common Stocks
Government Bonds	Corporate Bonds	Stock Mutual Funds
Fixed Annuities	R.E.I.T.s	"Speculative" Real Estate
Insured Municipal Bonds	MLPs	Junk Bonds
	BDCs	
	Indexed Annuities	

Source: CCG

greed model. Common stocks are what you normally think of when you hear the word "stocks." Dividend paying stocks also fall under this category, which is why you should avoid them. Stock mutual funds, naturally, are mutual funds that deal in these investments. You should avoid these as well. Commodities, meanwhile, are ultra-volatile, and unless you're dealing with any other real estate besides your home, you should probably avoid that as well.

On the other end is the more conservative end. Certificates of deposit are essentially the equivalent of cash. They pay you hardly anything and don't even match the rate of inflation, so you actually lose money for tying your money up in these. Government bonds are things like Treasuries, which, as we've discussed, also yield a paltry dividend—nowhere near enough to meet your retirement expenses. Municipal bonds are debt obligations usually issued by public entities such as cities and towns to fund infrastructure projects such as hospitals, highways, and schools. I'll go into the different types of annuities later on, but some are riskier than others.

That leaves the middle: the moderate risk. This includes corporate bonds, preferred stock, real estate investment trusts, master limited partnerships, business development companies, and certain kinds of annuities. I'll go into each of these in depth.

I said before that we want to get as close to zero risk as possible. Selecting investments at the "moderate" risk level, therefore, might seem counterintuitive. If our goal is to risk next to nothing, shouldn't we rather stick with conservative investments instead, such as government and municipal bonds and certificates of deposit?

In an ideal world, we would.

The reality is that these investments pay next to nothing. In the past, you could fund a decent retirement on these vehicles. Today, it's nearly impossible. Government bonds yield just one or two percentage points, municipal bonds rely on payments from over-indebted cities such as Chicago and Puerto Rico, and CDs pay as close to zero as you can get. Fixed annuities are really the only investment vehicle in this category that are worth your time.

The problem is, you can't fund your retirement with just one investment. Diversification is key. If you tie up all your money in one place and something goes wrong, you're out of luck. These investments may be conservative in nature, but no investing comes without some degree of risk, and something can always happen. These vehicles also have certain limitations I will get into a bit later.

So, since we don't have enough conservative investment options to effectively fund our retirement, we have to go for the next best thing. In the hands of a careful portfolio manager, moderate-risk investments can be almost as safe as conservative ones. We have just those kind of people working for us at Arbor Financial.

AIMING FOR 5 PERCENT

I'll get into each of these investment products in greater depth. But first, it's important to set our expectations for the amount of income we can expect to see each year.

We've discussed that historically, stocks give off 8 to 10 percent each year over a period of many, many years. In some years, like this past one, it will be closer to 20 percent or greater. In others, we may lose as much as 50 percent in a single year with stocks.

The problem is that if you want to shoot for that 8 to 10 percent range, you have to accept a potentially significant level of risk. There's no avoiding that. You can't get something for nothing. By shooting for that range, you have to be willing to accept that you might lose. You may be up big one year, and down even more the next.

So, we aim for a more reasonable figure.

Rather than shoot for 8 to 10 percent, we shoot for 4 to 7 percent. That is the annual yield we aim to achieve via our moderate and conservative portfolio of income-producing investments.

For the sake of simplicity, I use 5 percent.

That is the return I aim to deliver for my clients each year.

Some years will be a little lower and some years will be a little higher, hence why we try to stay in that range of 4 to 7 percent.

But, by aiming for a closer target rather than one that is far away, we don't miss our mark often, and when we do, it's typically not by much.

Even a skilled marksman will miss his target some of the time if his target is 100 yards away. He'll likely miss more often than he hits. He may only hit a bull's-eye once every 10 or 15 shots.

However, if we move that target much closer, to say 50 yards, he'll hit it almost every time. He may miss every now and then. But the number of times he hits it will more than make up for it. He'll still be able to maintain a steady, consistent, and overall impressive average.

He may not be as daring or as interesting as the marksman who prefers to take his chances at 100 yards. But if your goal is to hit your target, he's taking a bet he likely can't win.

That's what our goal is.

We're trying to avoid taking big bets. Our investments in our later age are supposed to be boring. When we enter retirement, we don't want to risk a thing.

THE DIFFERENT KINDS OF INVESTMENTS

I'll go through each of the investments I listed earlier in the "moderate" column. These are the investments that, when we sit down to map out your financial goals, we'll focus on, in order to meet those goals. Some of these are a little bit more complicated than others and some you may never have heard of, so I may spend more time on some than others.

PREFERRED STOCKS

Preferred stocks aren't what you normally think of when you hear the word "stocks." As I mentioned before, that usually refers to common stocks. There are some differences between the two but also some similarities.

Preferred stocks, like common ones, technically fall under the category of "equities," meaning they aren't bonds. However, these particular investments trade a little like bonds even though that's not what they technically are. Basically, they're a hybrid. Which is why they fall in the middle category of risk.

Common stocks, like preferred stocks, trade on the open market. Where they differ is that common stocks come with unique voting rights. As a common shareholder in a company's stock, you have a say in that company's decision making when it comes to running the business. Essentially, you own part of the company.

A preferred stock, however, doesn't come with unique voting rights. You don't own a part of the company. Essentially, you own a debt obligation. Rather than reward you with a part of the company that rises and falls in value with the company's performance, preferred stocks pay out a dividend that is usually higher than you can find in most bonds, even junk bonds, which are the highest paying, lowest quality bonds. These dividends can be as high as 6, 7, or even

8 percent depending on which company is the one issuing them (obviously, the higher the yield, the riskier the investment). Preferred stocks can still rise and fall in value depending on how the company is doing. But they're nowhere near as volatile as common stocks.

Common stocks sometimes pay a dividend, but sometimes they don't. The ones that don't are usually companies that are invested in still growing their business. Once the company reaches a certain size and wants their stock to be a little less volatile, they begin issuing a dividend to get investors to stick around. That's why dividend-paying stocks are indeed a little less risky than common stocks that are more focused on growth, but they still fall in the aggressive category.

So, if dividend-paying stocks and preferred stocks both pay a dividend, what's the difference?

The dividend on preferred stocks, as I mentioned, is often much higher—higher than that even of bonds. Since they're slightly riskier than bonds, that makes sense—you get rewarded more for putting up with more risk.

Preferred stocks are also much higher on the list of benefits.

While preferred stock holders don't own a share of the company per se, and therefore don't have voting privileges, voting privileges don't matter unless you have a sizeable stake in the company anyway, like several hundreds of thousands or even millions of shares. Honestly, what do you care what the company is doing anyway so long as it pays you? Preferred stocks also are much less risky because sometimes a company may temporarily pause its dividend payments. When this happens, common stockholders are out of luck—they're out of a dividend. For preferred shareholders, however, a company *can* pause their payments to these shareholders, but once they reissue the dividend, they have to pay them *before* common shareholders, and any dividend payments they missed they have to make up for.

So, let's say Ford Motor Company paused its dividend for six months. Both shareholders would be without payment during that time. However, once Ford resumes its dividend after six months, it has to pay preferred shareholders all the dividend payments they missed—all six months' worth. It doesn't have this obligation to common shareholders. Common shareholders likely wouldn't get paid a red cent.

So, preferred stocks are less risky than common stocks, and while they may not increase in value as much as a common stock when a company does well, they won't fall as far when a company does poorly. Not only that, they pay a set dividend each year.

But I also mentioned that preferred stocks behave a little like bonds and are slightly riskier.

Bonds are basically a debt obligation. Rather than purchase a stock from the company, with a bond, a company *borrows* money from you—money they'll pay back at a later date. In return for this favor, bonds come with monthly, quarterly, or annual dividend payments.

The difference on the payment ladder is that bondholders get paid *first*. While a company can suspend dividend payments for any of its shareholders, whether preferred or common, they cannot suspend dividend payments toward bondholders. That makes them less risky.

However, bonds fluctuate wildly with interest rates.

As interest rates rise, the value of a bond falls. That's because bonds that pay more aren't worth as much. Consider the case of U.S. Treasuries. Today Treasuries are in a bubble. They are at some of the highest levels they've been in years, because individual investors and our very own and even overseas governments have bought so many of them. With so many debt obligations, the government can't afford to pay any more than a small dividend of just 1 or 2 percent to these bondholders, depending on the duration of the bond.

Ironically, even though preferred stocks are often considered riskier than bonds, in this case they're actually safer. Preferred stocks do tend to decrease in value as interest rates rise. That's because they essentially work as bonds, paying off a dividend in response to a debt obligation. But because preferred stocks also fluctuate in value depending on how the company is doing, they aren't as totally influenced by interest rates as bonds are.

Common stocks move up or down depending on how the company is doing.

Bonds move up or down largely because of interest rates.

Preferred stocks do both. They're more diversified. And in that sense, they're in some ways safer.

I should point out as I did earlier on in the book that I believe we can expect interest rates to stay lower for longer. The Fed has been in a tightening cycle for nearly two years and interest rates have barely budged. They won't return to "normal" for a long, long time. Probably not until both you and I have passed.

A NOTE ABOUT RISK

Preferred stocks don't come without risk. These investments also fared poorly during the 2008 crash. But that's because it was a global *financial* crisis, meaning all financial securities suffered.

If we suffer from a similar kind of crisis the next time the market starts to crash, where liquidity dries up and there's not enough money available, we'll act accordingly and only target the safest preferred stocks if any at all. But for right now and throughout your retirement, preferred stocks can be ideally suited to individual investors who are seeking retirement income. They're less volatile than common stocks, and less subject to interest-rate rises than bonds. We can help you select the best ones.

CORPORATE BONDS

There are many different kinds of bonds. There are bonds that come from our nation's government. There are bonds that come from state governments and even cities. And there are bonds that companies directly issue. Each one is similar but come with a different set of circumstances, benefits, and risks. We'll focus on corporate bonds today because they pay more than the other two types and are less risky than many municipal bonds.

As mentioned, a bond is a debt obligation. You give the company money to fund a project, and while they hang onto it, they pay you a dividend for your service. Once the bond expires or you sell it, you get your money back plus all the dividend payments you received. Basically, it's a loan.

Bonds are boring. They're one of the most predictable investments in the book. They're the quintessential retirement vehicle—what they lack in excitement they make up for in reliability. But corporate bonds have a bit of flair that the others don't.

Since companies are all about growing and staying in business, they can afford to pay out higher dividends because they're more competitive. A city government, on the other hand, isn't as concerned with growing in power (at least on paper). Plus, politicians are usually incompetent. They don't know how to manage money, so they can't afford to pay out that much to those who invest with them. And while government bonds are usually backed by "the full faith and credit of the U.S. government," there have been several cases where bondholders have gotten ripped off.

Companies are typically better at managing money than politicians and governments, so paying bond investors a higher dividend works right into their business.

That said, corporate bonds are considered to be higher risk than government bonds because they aren't backed by the full faith and credit of the U.S. government. If the company goes out of business and has to liquidate assets and send the proceeds to investors, then corporate bondholders are at the top of the ladder — in front of preferred stockholders and the common stockholders behind them. In other words, they get paid first. But there's always the chance the company will be so deep in a hole that no one will get paid, including bondholders. It doesn't always happen, but it can happen.

That said, while most governments are over their heads in debt, some companies are not.

Many companies have borrowed money hand over fist to buy back a bunch of their stock and inflate their stock prices. But some companies have sound business practices that bondholders can rely on. Those are the companies bond investors need to target. Businesses that are using weird accounting practices to make earnings and revenue seem better than they are aren't ideally suited for investors who are just looking for income. But if you can find a corporate bond that pays a high dividend and that is tied to a company that is financially sound, it's one of the best retirement bets you can get. Considering interest rates won't rise very high anytime soon, corporate bonds can offer a steady 4 percent interest or more with a lot less volatility than the stock market.

REITS

Real estate can be speculative. We have seen the housing crash when housing prices fell some 18 percent in 2008. But real estate can also be one of the most secure investments there is.

That makes real estate investment trusts, or REITs, a rather interesting investment, especially for retirees.

While REITs deal in land and property, they trade just like stocks and often come with a very substantial dividend yield. Often compared to mutual funds, they give both large and small investors the opportunity to profit from large commercial properties such as apartment complexes, shopping malls, office buildings, medical facilities, warehouses, and even hotels. The fact is, there's money in these enterprises, and REITs are one of the easiest ways to take advantage of them.

It's a thriving business too. The SEC reports there are at least 200 REITs trading on a major exchange. They account for about $1 trillion in business.

Congress established REITs in the 1960s in order to bring opportunities in real estate to everyone. Because of their tax filing, these investment vehicles are required to deal out 90 percent of their revenues to investors, making them a favorite among income investors. Hence, they sport yields anywhere between 5 and even 11 percent!

REITs come with some level of risk. If you're buying mall REITs, you may have to suffer through some short-term volatility as many malls go out of business. That said, even as malls close, the land is still theirs. It will be used for other purposes. If that purpose serves some productive end—say a new, popular business that earns sky-high revenues—those REITs should continue to perform well. But, like any security that trades like a stock, REITs have one other advantage in our present environment. Most high-dividend-paying securities are expected to drop in value as the Federal Reserve raises interest rates. I've already explained why that's not a tremendous cause for concern since rates will stay lower for longer. But unlike other income investments, REITs can actually do *better* when interest rates are rising.

Rates tend to rise when the economy is improving. When the economy improves, people spend money on material luxuries. That includes property. Hence, REITs can actually do better when rates are rising because REITs, like any security that trades like a stock, tend to go up in value while the economy is rising. Higher rates may increase their funding costs, since these businesses borrow a lot of money which costs interest, but rising property values can more than make up for this.

MASTER LIMITED PARTNERSHIPS (MLPS)

Like REITs, master limited partnerships, or MLPs, are securities that pay high dividends and trade like stocks. Whereas REITs deal with real estate, MLPs often deal in the energy sector. And whereas REITs are required by law to distribute 90 percent of their cash to investors, MLPs have to distribute *all* of it. They're cash cows. For that reason, they offer some of the highest dividend payments you can get. Plus, they pay no federal taxes, meaning the amount of cash they can pay out is even greater.

The downside with these investments is that their value relies heavily on the energy sector since that's where 99 percent of them operate. When oil prices crashed between 2014 and 2016, MLPs fell through the floor. MLPs did very well for investors before oil prices crashed, rising in value and paying off massive dividends, and they've fared well since but are beginning to slump as oil remain volatile. We recommend them given their high dividends and considering oil prices are still cheap, though we don't suggest they take up a large portion of one's retirement portfolio in the off-chance they take another drop. Again, diversification is key.

BUSINESS DEVELOPMENT COMPANIES (BDCS)

These ones work a little different. Business development companies, or BDCs, do what their name suggests. They invest in and help small- to medium-sized businesses in the beginning stages of development. However, many still operate as publicly traded companies and trade on major exchanges, making investing in them as easy as finding the ticker symbol.

BDCs are another type of fund that were started by Congress in the 1980s. The goal was to provide financially distressed companies financial assistance in the early stages and also help fuel job growth. Not only do they offer financial help, they offer business advice to these startup firms. Considering 90 percent of startups fail, this sort of support can mean the difference between a multimillion dollar firm and hundreds of thousands of startup costs in debt.

Since BDCs are set up as investment companies, they are required to send out 90 percent of their profits to shareholders, which results in above-average dividend yields. Historically, their yields average 8.7 percent, higher than corporate or even junk bonds. It's important to bear in mind, however, that since BDCs can be volatile, their value can increase or decrease much more rapidly than, say, preferred stocks, corporate bonds, or even REITs. That said, they offer a much better risk/ return tradeoff compared with more aggressive securities such as junk bonds and common stocks. Over the last several years they have been significantly less volatile than small-, medium-, or even large-cap stocks.

ANNUITIES

Annuities are a completely different animal than anything we've just discussed. Whereas everything else I just mentioned (with the exception of corporate bonds) is publicly traded on the U.S. stock exchange, annuities are sold by insurance companies.

There are two different kinds—fixed and indexed annuities. Both provide you the opportunity to grow your money and build your retirement savings while protecting those funds from a downturn in the market. Additionally, they remove the "nest egg" equation. Rather than concern yourself with an amount you need to retire, annuities offer you a monthly income paid over the course of your life. But one of these annuities is riskier than the other.

A fixed annuity is the least risky of the two and actually falls under the "conservative" investment category. A fixed annuity is basically a contract between you and the insurance company. In exchange for a lump sum of capital (usually hundreds of thousands of dollars though not necessarily that high), the insurance company agrees to pay you a fixed rate of return for the rest of your life. Like Social Security, you can set the date you want payments to begin, which will affect the amount you receive each month. These are called "immediate" and "deferred."

Immediate fixed annuities allow a client to begin receiving payment the moment they open up the contract. Deferred fixed annuities, meanwhile, can be pushed to a later date.

The real upside of fixed annuities is that you know exactly what you get. You put money in, you get money out. Not only do these investments deliver a much better rate of return than say a bank CD, they make it convenient for you to be able to spread a lump sum of cash over the rest of your days on this earth. To pay for this convenience, the insurance company keeps the money and pays it back to you overtime at a fixed rate of return. The convenience for receiving a guaranteed income for as long as you live is a pretty good deal.

There are a couple risks, however.

Let's say you opt to begin receiving payments at age 65. You expect to live to be 90, but an aggressive form of cancer kills you at age 67. I don't mean to get dark, but it's a possibility, and retirement is all about weighing the possibilities and planning for the worst so you can avoid it.

Instead of receiving income for 25 years, you receive it for two. You have a couple of options to prepare for this scenario.

One, you elect for payments to stop when you die. You'll receive a higher rate of interest, meaning you'll get more money from the insurance company each month. You hope to see 25 years of income higher than what you would otherwise get, but you accept that you may not live that long. It's all about weighing the odds.

The other option is that you elect a beneficiary to begin receiving payments when you die. Most people elect their spouse. Once their spouse dies, the payments stop, period. The hope is that at least *one* of you gets to live a long, happy life, otherwise your investment didn't pay off.

But you can select other beneficiaries as well or even multiple beneficiaries. Each selection raises or reduces your costs, meaning you receive more or less each month.

An annuity is the exact opposite of life insurance. Life insurance is for people who die too early. Annuities are for people who live a long time. If you elect to have payments end after you die, make sure you have a life insurance policy taken out to support your family after you go. Otherwise, you can build that same type of policy into your annuity and have payments delivered to a beneficiary.

Fixed annuities are just one type of investment vehicle. The other, riskier kind is an indexed annuity, but even these qualify as "moderate" level investments.

Whereas fixed annuities provide a fixed, monthly payment for a lump sum of cash, indexed annuities and how they calculate their rate of return are dependent on the stock market going up. Your principal is guaranteed, and your gains are locked in at various anniversaries. This can be very beneficial. Stock market volatility becomes your friend and enhances your potential rate of return because the indexed annuity and its growth point will reset where the stock market lands. So if the market drops, the least you can earn is zero. Like fixed annuities, indexed annuities offer a guaranteed rate and minimum rate of return, normally around 1 percent over the contract term. However, since indexed annuities are tied to the stock market, you have the opportunity to earn much more or much less than you can with a fixed annuity. Personally, I recommend fixed annuities when interest rates are much higher. In today's rate environment, fixed annuities are not very attractive, while indexed annuities are good for middle-aged investors and retirees who cannot afford a stock market correction.

Presently, there are more than 630 variations of indexed annuities, and they tend to fall into two categories. One being *appreciation cen-*

tric, where they give you the largest share of the stock market growth and in some instances all of it based on its investing style.

The second style of fixed indexed annuities are *income centric*. Meaning they focus on the creation of guaranteed lifetime income that is built over time based on a specific compounded rate of interest between 5 to 7 percent. However, you sacrifice all your future growth in the stock market because crediting strategies limit what you can earn. You will only average between 1 to 3 percent on your money. This should be unacceptable to most. The problem is the majority of financial advisors advocate this type of indexed annuity for their clients. The reality is, only 10 to 15 percent of all annuity contract owners of these types of *income centric* programs will actually activate the guaranteed lifetime income component. The result is you cannibalize your principal. The insurance company is banking on paying you back your money first and is playing an actuarial game that favors the insurance company. These types of fixed indexed annuity programs are the ones you see advertised on TV, and I warn my clients and consumers to avoid them. This also applies to variable annuities where the fees can range from 2.5 to 4 percent annually. No financial strategy is perfect. The financial environment today has made planning for retirement more difficult than it's been in years, perhaps decades. Conservative bonds that once offered a competitive yield now are overpriced and barely cover expenses. Pensions are disappearing, and Social Security is running out of steam. Investors looking for income have been forced into riskier investments like junk bonds and common stocks. There is a better way.

The financial landscape offers a variety of alternative investments retirees today can use to fund a luxurious retirement. Preferred stocks offer income investors a competitive alternative to traditional bonds and common stocks. Corporate bonds beat similar investments by a mile. REITs, MLPs, and BDCs offer an incredible risk/reward advantage. Fixed annuities ensure retirees have the income they need to last their entire life.

While traditional investments no longer cut it, there are still plenty of options to choose from. Wall Street just isn't interested in showing them to you. Conservative or even moderate investments don't earn them as much.

That doesn't mean you have to settle for more risk and less income.

At this point, it's important to take a close look at your retirement strategy:

- How much income do you need each year to maintain your current or desired lifestyle in retirement?
- What rate of return do you need to earn each year to keep your assets intact and make sure that annual withdrawals don't cut into your principal?
- What level of risk are you willing to accept? Do you want to shoot for more aggressive yields such as those that BDCs and MLPs offer? Are REITs more to your liking? What about corporate bonds and preferred stocks? Can you combine higher yield investments with lower yield ones to find an overall average that meets your retirement needs?

Retiring isn't easy. It never has been. But it doesn't have to be impossible. There are plenty of options available to you if you're willing to embark on the road less traveled and leave Wall Street's way of doing things behind. Make sure your financial adviser understands this. Ask him how he'll invest your money. Drill him on the investments we've just covered. Ask him how he feels about risk. Is he willing to chase a slightly higher rate of return for a greater degree of risk, or is he willing to pursue a more reasonable goal that he knows he can hit? This is your retirement money. You can't afford to leave it in the hands of someone who won't keep you safe. You deserve a good retirement. We'll help you get it.

6

Making Social Security
Work for You

ONE OF THE most common questions I get whenever I sit down with a new client is this: "Will I be able to rely on Social Security in retirement?" The answer: yes and no.

Social Security is a complicated topic with lots of variables. For one, there's filing. When is the best time to file for benefits? What is the best time to begin receiving them? Then there's the whole matter of whether or not Social Security will even be around long enough for any of this to matter.

If you expect to begin collecting Social Security within the next 10 to 15 years, rest your worries: Social Security will in all likelihood be around exactly as it is today. But you should in no way, shape, or form, look to Social Security as your *primary* source of retirement income.

That's why I say yes and also no to the question of whether or not you can rely on it. You can, just not fully. It will be a different matter for your children, but for now, that's a problem for tomorrow.

The fact is, Social Security should not be viewed in a vacuum. It should not be your sole source of income in retirement. I say that knowing good and well that the statistics show the vast majority of people do in fact heavily rely on it for most if not all of their income. According to the Social Security Administration, some 52 percent of married couples and 74 percent of unmarried retirees get half or more of their retirement income from Social Security. But that's not the worst of it: some 22 percent of married couples and 47 percent of unmarried persons rely on it for 90 percent or more of their income.

Make no mistake: we are dealing with a retirement crisis here in America. But that doesn't mean you have to suffer the same fate. Statistics ultimately mean nothing to individual people. The goal of this chapter is to begin to show you how to maximize your Social Security benefits and how to incorporate them into your long-term financial strategy, so you can walk away with a more holistic plan for retirement.

SOME FACTS AND FIGURES

Let's start off with a few statistics from the Social Security Administration:

- The elderly, on average, rely on Social Security for 34 percent of their retirement income—so about a third. But as we saw above, some rely on it more than others.
- In 2017, over 62 million Americans will receive approximately $955 billion in Social Security benefits. That's close to $1 trillion each year. That's a large pie you get to have a piece of. Divide it out, and that's $15,403 per person. The reality is, your benefit can be much lower—and much greater—than that depending on if you play your cards right.
- Back when Social Security first started, life expectancy was so low you were lucky to even get to claim Social Security. Today, life expectancy is about 85 for both sexes. Meaning that you can expect to claim Social Security benefits for approximately 20 years. (But again, you're not a statistic! You could die at 62. Or you could live to be 100.)

- By 2035, the number of Americans age 65 and above will increase from approximately 48 million today to over 79 million—a jump of more than 50 percent. As we discussed in earlier chapters, America is aging, alongside the rest of the developed world.
- To go along with that previous fact, today there are 2.8 workers for each Social Security beneficiary, on average. By 2035, that number will drop to 2.2, meaning there will be just over two workers for every retiree, compared to just under three workers today.

Based on current trends, the U.S. government and the Social Security Administration will have to take a long, hard look at the program to make sure it's still around in the same or similar form for the long-term future. At this point, Social Security is running a deficit, meaning more funds are going out than funds are coming in. As time goes on and there are fewer workers per beneficiary paying into the system, the problem will only grow worse.

In 2010, the Social Security Administration began responding to this problem by withdrawing interest from the trust fund to make up for the gap.[11] By 2021, they won't just need to withdraw interest—they'll have to start cutting into the principal as well. If that's the route they take, by 2034, the trust funds are predicted to run out of money.

That's still some 16 or 17 years away. Just like you have to make sure your money and your income last into your later years, the Social Security Administration has the same problem. Unfortunately, the government isn't the best when it comes to financial sustainability, as our $20 trillion debt shows only too well. But, even if Social Security runs out of money, the amount they take in from taxes is enough to cover approximately 75 percent of all current benefits. So, in the worst case scenario, in your much later years, there's a possibility your benefits will drop by a quarter. Big deal. If you prepare for retirement the way I've advocated you do in this book, you'll barely notice the difference.

The biggest concern for you when it comes to Social Security is deciding when you wish to begin receiving benefits. But it's so much more complicated than just that.

If I asked you how many different ways there were to apply for Social Security, what number would you throw at me?

Ten?

Twenty?

One hundred?

You'd be wrong. Believe it or not, there 567 different ways to apply for Social Security. If you do it the wrong way, you could be out thousands and even tens of thousands of dollars in benefits each year—and hundreds of thousands over the course of retirement. Apply the right way, and that's money that goes straight into your pocket.

The first issue to contend with is income. If you have a $2 million portfolio at age 65 and elect to spend your 5 percent every year instead of investing it, that means you have $100,000 to live on each year. With that kind of income, it almost doesn't matter when you decide to start receiving Social Security. You're already set. You can elect to delay payments as long as you want to get the maximum payment whenever you choose to accept it.

If, however, you only have a $500,000 portfolio at age 60, you have some tough decisions to make. You'll be fine either way. With the 5 percent rule and any money you collect from Social Security, you'll be able to provide yourself with a fair (if perhaps modest) retirement. But with retirement around the corner and depending on how you apply for Social Security, you could be looking at a difference of several hundred or even thousands of dollars in income each month, which for you will make the difference between that more modest retirement, or a more comfortable one. This chapter is really for you.

This is what I mean when I say that Social Security must fit into your holistic, long-term retirement plan. You can't look at Social Security in a bubble. You need to figure out your income needs, for each year of retirement, and file for Social Security benefits from there, with an emphasis on receiving the highest possible benefit.

I've read that there are 567 different ways for a couple to claim Social Security. It's such a complicated and difficult matter to approach, with so many different variables, that only 18 percent of couples make any plans to maximize their benefits.[12]

Pat yourself on the back. Today, you join those ranks.

It's no secret that if you begin collecting Social Security payments early, you'll receive less per month than you would if you waited to receive them later. But that doesn't mean later is better than earlier, or that earlier is better than later. Fact is, there is only *one* right strategy for you. This is why it's so important to sit down and plot out this course with a trusted financial advisor who is concerned with making sure you receive your highest benefit.

EXAMPLE 1

Let's just dive into a couple of examples first.

Fred and Patricia are a married couple. Fred is about to turn 70 and Patricia is 65. Fred was a high-wage earner throughout his whole career and is entitled to receive the maximum Social Security benefit. For someone reaching full retirement age in 2018, that benefit would equal roughly $2,700.

However, while Fred *filed* for Social Security several years ago, he delayed the start of his payments until age 70. When a retiree elects to delay their payments, the amount they'll eventually receive each month grows by 8 percent every year. Sure, that means they'll collect less money now, but they'll collect more money later, per month, if they choose to take this route.

In Fred's case, since he's about to turn 70, he can begin collecting about $3,600 each month—$900 more each month than if he had begun collecting Social Security much earlier.

But then there's Patricia. At age 65, Patricia has her own decision to make. Patricia wasn't a high-wage earner like her husband, but she still brought in $75,000 per year. If she chooses to begin collecting Social Security now, she'll bring in about $1,800. Between that and Fred's $3,600 income from Social Security, they're looking at a total amount of $5,400 per month just from Social Security. That's $64,800 annually.

But Patricia has another option. As her husband's spouse, Patricia can choose to take advantage of her spousal benefit, collecting half of what Fred was eligible to receive when he received full retirement age. That benefit was roughly $2,700, so Patricia will collect half that, or about $1,350. It's less than the $1,800 she could collect on her own, but here's the catch. *(See note at the bottom of page 143.)

Rather than lose that extra money, Patricia elects to delay her benefit under her own work record. In other words, she can continue to collect the spousal benefit while her own benefit grows at 8 percent each year. When she turns 70, she'll be able to collect approximately $2,400 under her benefit. By that point, Fred and Patricia will pull in about $6,000 each month from Social Security, or $72,000 each year.

This is obviously a best case scenario. Fred was in the highest wage bracket and his wife also brought in a respectable income. Their age difference also meant that Patricia could delay payments on her own benefit while she collected her spousal benefit.

Whether or not their situation reflects yours, there are a few of takeaways from this:

1. Delaying payments from the time you reach full retirement age (66) means your monthly benefit will grow by 8 percent each year.
2. If you have a spouse and you both are eligible to receive Social Security, one can collect their benefit while the other collects a

spousal benefit and allows their own benefit to grow at the 8 percent annual rate. *

There are of course other factors to consider. How long do you expect to live? If you expect to live to be 85, 90, 95, or even 100, delaying Social Security so you can receive the maximum benefit later makes the most sense so you'll get more out of the program than if you elected to begin receiving payments earlier. On the other hand, if you have decent income from other investments and only plan to live until 80 (since it's ultimately a question of chance and fate), electing to receive payments earlier might make the most sense for you. I've worked with families that have tried both strategies. What works for one may or may not work as well for the other. It's important to remember, however, that if you elect to receive your benefits at the earliest age of 62, you are only eligible for 75 percent of your full retirement benefit, so there are drawbacks to accepting payments early. Likewise, if a spouse accepts his or her spousal benefit at age 62 instead of 66, he or she will only collect 35 percent of the spouse's full retirement benefit, rather than 50 percent.

EXAMPLE 2

Knowing a bit more about the different ways to apply for Social Security, let's look at another example.

Reggie has been a middle earner all his life. He pulls in $80,000 from his wages a year and at age 62, he's ready to file for Social Security, though not sure if he'll elect to begin receiving benefits now, at his full retirement age of 66, or the higher threshold of 70. His wife, Claire, age 60, worked a total of 8 years prior to raising their three children (you

---

* This is only true if both you and your spouse were both 62 on April 1, 2016. If you were not age 62 before these dates, there are other strategies you can take advantage of to maximize your social security benefits.

have to work 10 years to be eligible), so she isn't eligible for Social Security, but can receive a spousal benefit.

Social Security, of course, won't be their primary form of income. Reggie has a military pension from his time in the U.S. Navy that pays him $25,000 each year, and a separate work pension that pays $15,000. In addition, he has $500,000 in assets, enough to pay him $25,000 at 5 percent of his principal each year without eating into the principal itself.

That's a total of $65,000. Adding Social Security, for Reggie and Claire, means the difference between a modest-to-comfortable retirement and a much more flexible one.

After sitting down with Arbor Financial, Reggie and Claire settle on a course of action. Reggie's maximum benefit at the full retirement age of 66 is $2,100 a month, or $25,200 a year. Two years later, when Claire reaches full retirement age, she'll be able to pull in half that through her spousal benefit, adding $12,600 to their income.

By that point, Reggie and Claire will be age 68 and 66 and pulling in $102,800. It's a respectable amount, but they decide they can do better.

Since Claire is limited to her spousal benefit based on her husband's full retirement age, the most she can ever get out of the system is $1,050. If they want to maximize their benefits, they'll have to delay Reggie's benefits until later. This means that Claire will start collecting social security at age 68, and Reggie will begin collecting at age 70. They'll have to go without Social Security for an additional two years since Reggie will elect NOT to receive benefits at age 66, but instead at age 70. Again, this only applies because Claire was not 62 prior to April 1, 2016, and Reggie was. So, pay attention to that April 1, 2016 date when calculating how to maximize your benefits; that's what we do for you at Arbor Financial. Since his benefit will grow at 8 percent per year post age 66 and Reggie can expect a monthly Social Security benefit of $2,850 each month or approximately $34,200 each year, which is $9,000 more each year, by allowing his Social Security to grow over those four years. That puts Reggie and Claire's total income at $111,800, and it gives Claire a higher death benefit in the event that Reggie predeceases her. (To date, a majority of husbands still pass away before their wives).

EXAMPLE 3

Let's look at one final example, because ultimately, as much as your unique Social Security situation may resemble one of these examples, your situation will likely be quite different with its own distinct variables.

Holly is a single mother of two, age 57. Her two boys are attending college, one on scholarship and another with some financial assistance from his mother. Holly brings in $60,000 a year as a nurse, has $300,000 in savings but has no other assets to speak of beside her home. She has $150,000 in home equity but owes $150,000 still on her mortgage, so it cancels out.

If Holly decides to retire early at age 62 she can collect $1,100 a month in Social Security or $13,200 annually. By that point she hopes to have her home fully paid off without tapping into her savings. Applying the 5 percent rule, Holly can expect to receive $15,000 in retirement income from her $300,000 portfolio. That's $28,200 a year she'll have to spend, which barely covers her living expenses and leaves little room for a nasty medical scare.

Knowing retiring at 62 is out of the question, Holly sets her sights on 65. By then, she can collect $1,500 a month in Social Security and hopes to have saved aggressively, growing her savings to $375,000. By delaying retirement those extra three years, Holly's total income will rise to $36,750. That's a 30 percent increase from her previous amount of $28,200 based on an earlier retirement age. She won't have a luxurious retirement by any means, but it will be enough to support her and comes out to about 75 percent of her current salary. Knowing she won't save as much during retirement, Holly decides it's doable. And if everything goes according to plan, she'll still be able to leave $200,000 to each of her two children.

Holly shows the importance of a holistic retirement strategy that looks at *all* of your sources of income. Her savings alone wouldn't cut it. Neither would Social Security. But together, these two income streams are enough to sustain her in retirement.

Hopefully you can take some lessons away from these three examples. The fact is, most people are leaving money on the table when it comes to Social Security. Don't worry about when the Social Security Administration will run out of money—that isn't your concern. They won't run out of money during your lifetime. You're legally entitled to as much as you're able to get based on how much you've paid into the system. It's your money, after all. And even if they're forced to make some changes, it will be so late into your well-thought-out retirement years that it won't even matter.

Remember, just because you file for Social Security at age 62 (or 65, or 66, or whenever you choose to file), you have no obligation to discontinue working. You can keep working to buffer up your retirement portfolio while your Social Security continues to grow to age 70.

ANOTHER TIP: if you're married and you want to make sure your spouse receives the most money if one of you passes away, try and delay claiming benefits until reaching the maximum age of 70. That way, the surviving spouse has a choice between their own monthly benefits or the full amount of their deceased spouse, whichever is higher. This is exactly the setup that Reggie and Claire elected in the second example. If Reggie passes before Claire, Claire won't be able to continue receiving both her and her deceased husband's benefits, but she can elect to receive his benefit instead of hers since his was higher, raising her entitlement from her small spousal benefit of $12,600 a year to $34,200 a year, a 171 percent increase on her benefit (a near triple!) and only a 27 percent decline on their total Social Security benefit as a couple.

7

To Sell or Not to Sell:

THE PROBLEM WITH REAL ESTATE

THE AVERAGE AMERICAN aged 65 years or older has $130,000 in home equity. For most Americans, their home is their single greatest asset. It's the largest purchase they'll ever make and for many it accounts for the vast majority of their net worth. It's a critical component of one's retirement strategy. Do you sell? Do you downsize? Do you rent? There are plenty of factors to consider, and there's no right or wrong way to go about them. Everyone's plan for their home will be different for different reasons. The goal for each of my clients that comes to me is to determine the best plan for them when it comes to their home.

First, it's important to recognize that a home isn't just an investment. Sure, you put money into it. If you're like 99 percent of the people out there, you've watched the value of your home rise and fall and then rise again over the past decade and probably wondered when is the best time to get out of the market if you haven't done so already.

But as an investment, the money you put into a home is different from the money you put into stocks. It's more complicated.

If you're a person who is calm, logical, and who values reason over emotion, it might be an easier subject to approach for you.

If you or anyone in your family is the other way around and takes a more sentimental approach to their home, it may be more difficult.

FIG. 20. Median Home Equity

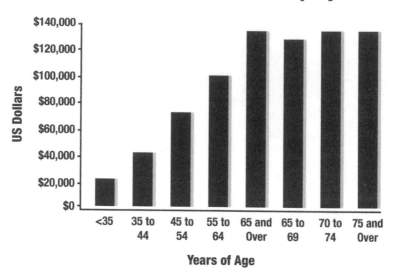

Source: Median Value of Assets for Households
https://www.census.gov/data/tables/2011/demo/wealth/wealth-asset-ownership.

When my wife and I bought our home, we wanted just that—a home. A house is a place you live. A home is a place where you raise a family and establish memories that will last for the rest of your life. My wife and I are unsure whether we'll sell our home in retirement. Personally, I suspect we'll sell it. As fond as our memories are of it, there's a lot of money in that house and it will be nice to be able to play with it in retirement.

That said, I'm still plenty of years away from retirement. I could work for another 10 to 20 years for all I know. I may change my mind when I get closer to retirement. To me, my home is in many ways still just a house. But my youngest children are still only five and seven. As I watch them grow up in their family home, memories will attach to the walls within it and I may find myself unable to part with it. My children, who are happy where they live, may I insist I not sell it.

I'm sure you have your own feelings about your home just as I do about mine. Those feelings might be that you don't have any feelings about it at all! Maybe your house is boring. Maybe it's a money pit and you'd rather get something nicer. Maybe you won't want to downsize when you retire. If you can afford it, maybe you'll want to upsize! Some retired couples do it. It's nice to have the extra space when friends and family come to visit.

The most important thing you can do about your home right now is to ask yourself, what does your home mean to you?

You've put anywhere from $200,000 to $1 million into it if you're the average American. It may be easy to rest knowing you have that much cash sitting inside a single asset. At the same time, it might make you feel *un*easy. That's especially true after Americans saw their homes crash as much as 30 percent when the housing bubble burst in 2006—even more in metropolitan areas.[13]

Now, just as stocks have climbed to record highs, home prices have climbed alongside them. Those who held onto their homes through the crash and have watched their homes return to their peak values and then some are experiencing two feelings right now. They're overjoyed their investment has paid off and protected their cash. But they don't want to risk losing a significant portion of it again.

Some cities, like Miami, New York, and Los Angeles, seem to be back in bubble territory. If any one of those markets crash, who knows what that will mean for the broader market? It may only affect those areas. But more likely, it will cause homes across the entire nation and even the world to take a hit. All it can take is for just one of those bubbles to pop.

I won't spend as much time in this chapter disputing the technical case for housing prices. I want to spend more time helping you determine what your home means to you and what you're willing to risk.

Let's consider a fictional example of a 65-year-old couple named Jack and Stephanie. Jack and Stephanie bought their home in the suburbs of Chicago 20 miles outside of the city for $200,000 back in the

1990s. By the mid-2000s their home's value had doubled to $400,000, only to crash to $300,000 when the bubble burst. They were still ahead on their investment, but it never feels good to know you could have $100,000 more than you do right now.

Today, Jack and Stephanie's home is worth more than it's ever been. They could sell it on the open market today for $500,000, which is two and a half times more than what they purchased it for 20 years ago.

Jack and Stephanie have a decision to make. They own their home outright. It's completely paid off. But Chicago's housing market is expensive. There's a chance it could be worth slightly more in the next five or even 10 years, but there's a greater chance it could be worth significantly less.

So, do they cash in and sell their home on the open market and downsize to a smaller home, apartment, or condo?

That depends on a number of factors.

Jack and Stephanie have $750,000 in their retirement account not including their home. If they sell their home today and purchase a cheaper one for $250,000, their retirement account would be worth $1 million. It's more than possible to retire on $750,000. But it's much easier and more fun to retire with $1 million.

That said, what kind of retirement do Jack and Stephanie wish to have? Are they comfortable staying put, traveling once or twice a year to visit their children but always returning to the home they spent most of their married life in? Or would they want to use the extra money to travel to various exotic destinations such as Rome, Machu Picchu, or Paris? Or would they really like to kick their retirement into high gear, sell their home, buy a boat for $250,000 and use it to sail around the world for a year? Those kinds of decisions are possible on a retirement of $750,000. But they're much more doable and cause less financial stress on a retirement worth $1 million.

How much does Jack and Stephanie's home mean to them? Their

house is worth $500,000. But their home, to them, is priceless. Jack and Stephanie have four kids and three grandchildren. Does it matter to them that their entire family can gather on holidays in the home their children grew up in? Or would it be just as meaningful gathering somewhere else? Ultimately, it's their decision, but it's one they may wish to include their entire family in on.

There's a lot to consider. Some couples are more sentimental about things like home and family or even furniture. Others are more free-spirited. There's no right or wrong way. Everyone has their own personality and lifestyle. It's up to you to determine what your values are and how your home plays a part in that.

Most couples aren't used to being treated this way by a financial adviser. Most advisers are very by-the-book, looking strictly at facts and figures and numbers and bullet points. I prefer to take a more human approach. Call me sentimental! But I realize that a home means something different to every couple.

Let's consider another couple named Paul and Diane.

Paul and Diane are both age 60. They have a more modest retirement set aside than Jack and Stephanie. Paul and Diane have $500,000 in their retirement account and $200,000 in home equity. They still have $100,000 on their mortgage. So, in total, their net worth is $600,000—less than half than that of Jack and Stephanie.

Both of them are still only 60 years old. And thankfully, Paul enjoys his job and is willing to work for another 10 years, though if he could retire in five years, he might. It's on the table.

While Paul and Diane aren't as prepared for retirement as Jack and Stephanie, their situation is actually much simpler. Paul and Diane's home is neither big nor flashy. They moved around a lot as Paul spent 20 years in the service. After that, they moved around a lot for work. Hence, Paul and Diane have only lived in their current home for 10 years. They don't have much emotional attachment to it, and neither do their two kids.

However, Paul and Diane have less to gain by selling their home than they do by keeping it. Their house is worth $300,000, but they also have a $100,000 mortgage. If they sold it on the open market today, they'd only gain $200,000. That's enough to rent a $1,200/month apartment for 15 years. They expect to live to 85 or 90. So to them, it's not worth selling their home. They might choose instead to invest $30,000 of their retirement into the home to remodel and refurnish it to their liking. It might even be a fun project Paul and Diane can invest their time in. Instead of investing for retirement, they'd be investing *in* it.

This is the irony of housing. Homes that are worth more are more precious to us and therefore more difficult to sell. Plus, if they have more memories attached to them, that makes it even harder.

Paul and Diane, however, don't have the financial freedom available to even think about selling their home. That's a different kind of freedom—the freedom from too many choices. For Jack and Stephanie, selling their $500,000 home could mean the difference between a modest retirement and a lavish one. It's enough of an investment to supercharge their retirement from $750,000 to $1,250,000. Paul and Diane, however, would have only $600,000 after paying off their mortgage. Their home plays a minimal role in their retirement, whereas for Jack and Stephanie it plays a big one. For them, it makes more sense to stay put, keep working, and put more money into the home so they can actually enjoy it. You'd be amazed at what a $30,000 renovation can do.

Perhaps Paul and Diane will choose to sell their home anyway and rent for a few years while Paul continues working. They're prepared to put $30,000 into their home anyway, so they can just as easily put that money toward rent. When they do retire, they'll have more than enough money to buy the home they want. If they choose to mortgage their home rather than pay for it in cash, it'll be an additional monthly expense, but by that point their retirement account, including the money they got from their original home, would have likely climbed to $1 million. Their monthly mortgage payment would just be a drop in the bucket, especially since I would be able to help them prop up their funds in retirement.

So, what does your personal and financial situation for your home look like?

Do you like your home? Do you view your house as a home or as an asset? What about your spouse? What about your children? Do they like it? Do any of you have any specific and meaningful memories attached to it that would make selling your home difficult?

What about your values? Do you wish to travel more in retirement? Do you want a central "hub" the kids and grandkids can all gather at for family reunions? Can you do that somewhere else?

The list of questions you need to ask yourself goes on and on.

Is it worth it to downsize your home? Should you set some of the equity in your home aside for retirement so it's safe and accessible to spend (or invest as the need arises) while putting the rest toward a smaller, more efficient home?

Is it worth renovating your current home? Would it be cheaper and less of a hassle to move somewhere else?

Does your current home require a lot of maintenance?

Are you still paying off your mortgage?

Is it a large home? Is it an old home? Older homes can be very expensive to maintain. And the larger it is, the more time and money you'll have to sink into it. If your A/C unit goes out on a mid-sized home, you're looking at a $5,000 replacement. If water damage has compromised the foundation of your home, you're looking at a $10,000 repair—minimum. Add property taxes and it might be worth it just to rent. (GOBankingRates.com says it costs as much as $1,204 to maintain the average home after accounting for taxes, utilities, insurance, and other expenses. That's not $1,204 every year. That's each month. You can rent a home for that!)

More broadly, does your current retirement plan rely on the equity in your home like it did for Jack and Stephanie? Would selling your home supercharge your retirement strategy and make your retirement more carefree and easier? Would it make up for the personal loss of selling your home? Or is your situation more like Paul and Diane's, where you home plays a small part, but isn't a significant factor in your overall retirement plan?

Would you feel more peace of mind if you sold your home? Should you consider renting for a few years to see if the housing market doesn't crash like it did leading up to the financial crisis? Would it make you feel better? This is an issue that is not discussed enough. A house is a big and expensive thing. It can place either a financial burden or provide financial security to the person who owns it.

Then there's the matter of location. *Where* is your home? Do you own property right smack dab in the middle of a big, metropolitan city? Do you live on the outskirts or suburbs of that city? Do you live at least 100 miles or more away from any such place? If the market ever crashes during your retirement, it will make a big difference whether you live in the heart of Chicago or a small town or rural community.

That's another question you need to ask.

Can you survive financially if your home drops 30 or 40 percent? If you only have $250,000 in retirement and $250,000 in home equity, you only have $500,000. You can retire on that but not as easily as someone like Jack and Stephanie or even Paul and Diane could. They might be able to suffer a 30 percent blow to their home. But if you only have half a million dollars including the equity in your home set aside for retirement, and your home falls 30 percent, you're looking at close to just $400,000 in total. And assuming the stock market falls along with the housing market like it did in 2008, you might be looking at less. All of this plays together.

It's also important to remember that you can exclude a large portion of the capital gains you earn if you sell your home. If you're single, widowed, or divorced and have lived in your home two out of the last five years, you can exclude up to $250,000 from the sale of your home. That money is tax free. If you're married, you can exclude up to $500,000. That's not the total value of the home. That's what you've made on the home since you've bought it. There aren't a lot of investments where you can make that kind of return tax free.

The fact of the matter is, many people are going into retirement today without enough money saved. If you don't want to get caught in a future housing crisis, selling while the market is hot may be wise.

I can't predict the future. I can't tell you whether the housing market will crash today or whether home prices will double in the next 20 years.

What I can tell you is that housing prices have never been more expensive than they are right now. This is where good old-fashioned common sense comes in. If something seems too good to be true, there's a chance that it is. Nothing in this life is free. If you've made a significant amount of money on your home and you've made it just by sitting there, it might be worth it to consider parting ways.

I can't tell you what to do with your home. I can tell you what makes sense. You ultimately have to decide for yourself what's right for you and your family. I'm leaning toward selling my home when I retire. I may change my mind at a later date.

Here are some hard and fast guidelines I can tell you now:

1. If you have a large home, it may be worth it to downsize. Perhaps you bought that home back when you were raising your children. Now all that extra space is only used when the grandkids come to visit. If you can afford that luxury, great. If it helps to sell your home and take the capital gains, it might be worth it to downsize. Smaller homes are not only less expensive, they're cheaper to maintain. Property taxes are less expensive, too. Fact is, if you're wasting crucial retirement funds

just to hang onto a little bit of extra space, and it would be worthwhile to put that money elsewhere, sell that sucker while the market is still hot.

2. If your home has stairs, you can do two things. Keep your body young and healthy so climbing them isn't an issue. Or move everything you need down to the first floor. If all the bedrooms are upstairs and you think stairs could become a burden in your old age, there's no question about it—you should sell. Sure, you could remodel your home to put a bedroom on the first floor. But it would be much, much easier to sell it and find a better one.

Conclusion

THANK YOU FOR taking the time to read this book. I hope it's been a useful, educational experience for you that, if nothing else, has gotten you thinking a little more carefully about your long-term retirement strategy.

While most of the big-name financial institutions tout risk as the be-all-and-end-all, the reality is that at a certain age, risk becomes a cancer to any portfolio. Buy-and-hold only works in long-term bull markets. It doesn't work in long-term bear markets or at the end of a long-term bull market. In the credit meltdown and financial crisis of 2008, every asset class failed and even U.S. Treasury bonds, one of the "safest" investments there is, dropped in value. Today, the stock market is more expensive than it's ever been. All these factors should lead you to one conclusion: it's time to "modernize" your portfolio and practice the art of financial self-defense.

I know I've spoken poorly of the financial advisers who work in my business and I did that for a reason. Many of them don't have your best interest at heart—they just want to get paid. But I do encourage you to work with a fiduciary, like myself, because they are required by law to put your needs ahead of their own. After reading this book, you have a better idea of what that kind of adviser should look like. If you're interviewing new advisers because you realize your current one won't cut it, ask him or her some of the questions I've posed here. Go to my website, arbor-financial.com, and pick up a copy of "What a fiduciary advisor looks like." This white paper should help you, but if you need more advice, simply call my office. I cannot overstate how *important* this is to a happy retirement. The difference could be hundreds of thousands of dollars to you and your family.

I once had a case of an 80-year-old widow who came to see me after a family member pointed out that something was fishy in one of her portfolios. She had given a stockbroker $200,000 to invest for income in 2012. In 2017, her principal had lowered to $120,000. He said he was giving her "income." What he was actually doing was investing her money in high-risk real estate. She didn't know any better. Why should she? Nobody ever advocated for her, and nobody certainly ever educated her—not at least in matters of finance.

Take her experience to heart. A lot of advisers and brokers don't do the right thing by their customers. Their sales practices are self-serving and do not put your needs ahead of their own. Use this book to practice more discretion next time you talk to your financial adviser. Make sure they're worth their salt. I have yet to meet a financial advisor who understands the right way to work with clients because the industry and the financial culture believe that risk is an acceptable component of managing client assets and that losing some of your money is okay. If your advisor believes risk is okay and that it's okay to lose your money, you need to switch your advisor immediately.

Let's run over a few key points before we wrap this up.

Be smart. Remember, past performance is no guarantee of future returns. Many smart people believe the market is highly overbought at today's levels. Some of the greatest minds in finance like Warren Buffett or John Bogle, the founder of Vanguard, think the market will grow maybe 4 to 5 percent over the next 10 to 15 years. By switching to an income-oriented strategy like the kind I can provide you at Arbor Financial, I can get you that type of return in interest or dividends with nowhere near as much risk.

Remember the difference between investing for growth versus income. Investing for growth is for youngsters or those who have money to throw away, hoping to score big. Investing for income is for retirees and pre-retirees who don't have the time, energy, or assets to continue playing the slots. Time is money. If you're 55 or older, the fact is, you don't have as much time as you used to. Don't throw your money and time away by betting on a poor risk-to-reward scenario. Get out of risk and lock in your gains now before it's too late.

Be smart. Remember all the variables that go into play when you're mapping out your long-term financial plan. The most important thing you can do is to maximize your income and not expose your assets to any undue risk. As I said earlier in the book, the "Goldilocks Zone" is 5 percent. Your net rate of return needs to average 5 percent. We can show you how. I consider it a privilege to have this time with you now and look forward to talking to you in the near future.

Factor in your home or your mortgage. Weigh in Social Security. Consider your health, your livelihood, and your family history. Consider your children. Consider your spouse. Most of all, consider yourself. You deserve to have a happy, carefree retirement to reflect on the incredible life you've lived. You owe that to yourself. And don't you dare let anyone ever take it away from you. It's your retirement. Make it worth it.

Index

Note: Page numbers in italics indicate figures.

American dream, 7–26
annuities, 132–35
Arbor Financial, 4, 22–23, 25, 117, 120, 158
auto industry, 58–59, 71

baby boomers, 63
    retirement of, 64, 67–68, 71
bear markets, 13–14, 45, 53, 55
benchmark interest rate, 78
Bernanke, Ben, 81–82
birth rate, falling, 59–60, 61–63, 66–71, 88
Bogle, John, 158
Brexit, 88
Buffett, Warren, 95, 158
bull markets, 12–13, 14, 22, 53, 56–57, 88
business development companies (BDCs), 131–32, 135, 136
"buy and hold," 11, 12, 15, 91, 157

capital gains, 155
capitalism, 102, 104
cell phones, 57–58

central banks, 77–78
certificates of deposit (CDs), 115
childcare costs, 62, 69–70
child-rearing
    costs of, 62–63
    subsidies for, 70
China, 68–69
    one-child policy in, 71
college tuition, costs of, 62, 63, 69–70
consumer advocacy, 10–11, 24, 29, 30–32, 36, 38–39, 40–41
corporate bonds, 127–29
corporate buybacks, 71–76, 73, 77, 85–86, 88
corporate earnings, 2
corporate handouts, 84–86
costs, 38–39, 47
    of college tuition, 62, 69–70
    medical, 5, 23, 37, 100, 159
    understanding, 27–28

deflation, 77–78
democracy, 102
demographic problems, 61–71. *See also* birth rate, falling
developed nations, low birth rates in, 66–69
discipline, teaching, 27–28

dividend stocks, 112–13
Dow Jones Industrial Average, 12, *12*,
    96, 116
    2000–2017, *85*
    history of, 92–93
downsizing, 155–56

economic downturns, 55. *See also* bear
    markets; *specific crises*
economic uncertainty, era of, 93–94
efficient market hypothesis, 51–52
Einstein, Albert, 15, 31–32
entitlement benefits, 103–8
entitlements, 28. *See also specific*
    entitlements
ethics, 40–41

"fake news," 5
fear, 46, 52
fed funds rate, 78–79
Federal Reserve System, 77–82, 113–15
financial advisors, 23–24, 36–39, 91,
    116–17, 157–58. *See also* financial
    planners
    motivations of, 96
    responsibility of, 55–56
financial advocates, 41
"financial blindness," 28–31
financial education, 32–33, 35–36
"financial engineering," 71–72, 88
financial literacy, 27–28. *See also* financial
    education
financial planners, 108, 109
financial planning, 2–4, 52–53
    done right, 38–39
    ethical, 4
    traditional model of, 35
    traditionally accepted standards of, 25
financial planning advice, 25–26
financial planning industry, 4, 9–11, 16,
    25, 107
    accountability in, 11
    fees, 16–22, 38–40
financial safety nets, 55

financial securities, 115
financial situation, 23
financial strategy, 42–45
    defensive, 6, 27–50, 34–35, 52, 55,
        90–91, 97, 157
5 percent, as magic number, 119–36
4 percent rule, 108–9
401(k)s, 106
Fuller, Ida May, 103
the future, planning for, 36–38

gambling, 1–2
General Electric, 96
getting more for less, 39–40
globalization, 88
Goldilocks zone, 77, 119–36
Goldman Sachs, 74–75
government bonds, *115*
government debt, 107, 108
Great Depression, 11, 93, 103
Great Recession of 2008, 11, 59, 70,
    74–75, 77, 78, 80, 90
greed, 52, 95
Greenspan, Alan, 12–13
gross government debt, *83*
growth, putting aside, 34–35

history, repetition of, 55
home equity, *148*, 154
housing bubble, 52, 149
housing crisis of 2007, 11
housing market, 149, 155
housing prices, 149
HSBC, 75

Illinois, 105
income
    in the age of quantitative easing (QE),
        113–17
    declining, 60
    income streams, 23
    retirement and, *33–34*
India, 68–69
industries, peaking of, 58–59, 71, 112

INDEX

inflation, 2, 61–62, 78
inflationary crisis of 1970s, 11
interest rates
  benchmark, 78
  low, 2, 88, 113–15
the Internet, 56–57
investing, 1–2
  for growth, *33–34*, 158
  for income, *33–34*, 158–59
investment risk, types of, 120–36
investments
  annuities, 132–35
  business development companies
    (BDCs), 131–32
  corporate bonds, 127–29, 135, 136
  different kinds of, 124
  master limited partnerships (MLPs),
    131
  preferred stocks, 124–27, 135, 136
  REITs, 129–30, 135, 136
IRAs, 106
"irrational exuberance," 12–13

Japan, 65–66
  "demographic time bomb in," 65–67
  gross government debt in, *83*
  negative interest rates in, 83–84
  QE in, 82–83
  stagnating wages in, 67

Kostin, David, 74–75

life expectancy, 5, 103, 105
Lynne, Gillian, 31

margin debt, 86–87, *87*
master limited partnerships (MLPs),
  131, 135, 136
the media, 24
medical costs, 5, 23, 37, 100, 159
Medicare, 100
millennials, 61, 64, 71
monetary policy, 77–80. *See also*
  quantitative easing (QE)

money market funds, 115

National Ethics Association, 4
natural gas industry, 71
negative interest rates, 83–84

oil industry, 71

pensions, 103–7, *106*
Perry, Rick, 82
personal computers, 56–57, 58
Pew Research, 68
population, 102
post-war boom, 93
preferred stocks, 124–27
pre-retirees, 117
progressive era, 93
property taxes, 156

quantitative easing (QE), 79–82, 83,
  99–118
  income in the age of, 113–17

real estate, 147–56
  guidelines, 155–56
  housing bubble, 52, 149
  housing crisis of 2007, 11
  housing market, 149, 155
  housing prices, 149
REITs, 129–30, 135, 136
retail industry, 59, *60*, 71
retirement. *See also* pensions
  crisis in, 100
  delaying, 53
  history of, 101–3
  "holistic approach," 110–12, 116–17
  income and, *33–34*
  new, 110–12
  as new phenomenon, 99
  planning for, 52–53
  preparing for, 3, 5, 22–23, 25–26,
    30–31
  savings for, 99–100, 107–8
  statistics, 99–100

statistics *(cont.)*
  taking back, 107–8
risk
  minimizing, *33*
  preferred stocks and, 127
  types of investment risk, 120–36
Roaring Twenties, 93, 103
Russell 3000, 95–96

S&P 500, 13, *13, 14, 76*
safety nets, 55
Sander, Bernie, 88
saving, 64, 99–100, 107–8
savings accounts, 115
self-reliance, 107
self-sufficiency, 107
smartphones, 57–58
Social Security, 5, 99–100, 104, 105–6,
  116, 137–46, 159
Social Security Administration, 68, 100,
  103, 137–39
South Dakota, 105
stagflation, 93
standard of living, 102, 105
stock cycle macro trends, *93*
stock market, 115–16
  booms, 93
  bubbles, 89 (*see also specific bubbles*)
  crashes, 45, 49, 53–54
  cycles of, 92–96, *93*
  direction of, 12–13
  exposure to, *3*
  getting out of the, 51–98
  history of, 92–96, *93*
  overpriced, 52
  playing the, 1–3
  predicting, 51
  recovery of, 11
  underperformance of, 95–96
stocks
  corporate buybacks, 71–76, 77
  overpriced, 71–72
  preferred, 124–27
  pricing of, 51–52

repurchasing of, 71–72
store closures, *60*
student debt, 70
support systems, 101

tech bubble of 2000, 11, 52, 70
technological innovations, 56–59, 64
10-year Treasury notes, 115
Trump, Donald J., 87
  election of, 2, 88, 116

United Kingdom, gross government debt
  in, *83*
United States, gross government debt
  in, *83*
U.S. 10-year government bond yield, *114*
U.S. Census Bureau, 68

Von Bismarck, Otto, 101

Wall Street Journal, 92
Wisconsin, 105
workforce, declining, 63–64

yield, importance of, 99–118

Endnotes

1. US Birth Rates since 1900: US Census Bureau and Pew Research Center, https://www.cdc.gov/nchs/, http://www.pewsocialtrends.org/2012/11/29/u-s-birth-rate-falls-to-a-record-low-decline-is-greatest-among-immigrants/

2. American Economy and the Average that Americans have in Savings, https://en.wikipedia.org/wiki/Economy_of_the_United_States, http://www.marketwatch.com/story/most-americans-have-less-than-1000-in-savings-2015-10-06

3. Cost of College and Ivy League Institutions, http://blog.collegetuitioncompare.com/2015/05/ivy-league-2015-2016-estimated-tuition.html

4. The Average Cost of Daycare for Children to the Age of 4, https://www.newamerica.org/in-depth/care-report/introduction/

5. Sending you child to a lower-end and higher-end college, https://trends.collegeboard.org/college-pricing/figures-tables/average-published-undergraduate-charges-sector-2016-17, https://www.usnews.com/education/best-colleges/paying-for-college/articles/2017-09-20/see-20-years-of-tuition-growth-at-national-universities

6. Russell 3000, The Capitalism Distribution - The Realities of Individual Common Stock Returns by Eric Crittenden and Cole Wilcox, BlackStar Funds, https://seekingalpha.com/article/108867-the-capitalism-distribution-fat-tails-in-motion

7. Social Security Benefits, http://time.com/money/4644332/maximum-social-security-benefit-2017/

8. Percent of American Workers Pensions, https://www.ssa.gov/policy/docs/ssb/v35n4/v35n4p10.pdf, http://www.ncpers.org/files/evolution_of_public_pensions_2d.pdf

9. Underfunded State Pensions, https://www.bloomberg.com/search?query=10+states+with+the+most+underfunded+pensions&endTime=2017-09-24T00:34:58.945Z&page=1

10. Median American Family Average, https://www.cnbc.com/2016/09/12/heres-how-much-the-average-american-family-has-saved-for-retirement.html

11. Funding Levels of Social Security, http://time.com/money/3967821/social-security-trust-fund-2034/

12. How Many Ways can a Couple Claim Social Security, http://www.bankrate.com/financing/retirement/567-ways-to-collect-social-security/

13. Housing Market Crash, http://www.aei.org/publication/free-fall-how-government-policies-brought-down-the-housing-market/, http://www.ncpa.org/pdfs/st335.pdf